MARIUSZ MOROZ

The Banners in the Battle of Grunwald

The Banners in the Battle of Grunwald by Mariusz Moroz
Cover image by Mariusz Moroz
Translated and edited by Vincent W. Rospond and Dariusz T. Wielec
Originally published in 2020
This English edition published in 2023

Winged Hussar Publishing is an imprint of

Winged Hussar Publishing, LLC
1525 Hulse Rd, Unit 1
Point Pleasant, NJ 08742

Copyright © Winged Hussar Publishing/Mariusz Moroz
ISBN HC 978-1-958872-20-8
LCN 2023940091

Bibliographical References and Index
1. History. 2. Poland/Germany. 3. Medieval

Winged Hussar Publishing, LLC All rights reserved
For more information
visit us at www.whpsupplyroom.com

Twitter: WingHusPubLLC
Facebook: Winged Hussar Publishing LLC

This book is sold subject to the condition that it shall not, by way of trade or otherwise, be lent, resold, hired out, or otherwise circulated without the publisher's prior consent in any form of binding or cover other than that in which it is published and without a similar condition, including this condition, being imposed on the subsequent purchaser.

The scanning, uploading, and distribution of this book via the Internet or via any other means without the permission of the publisher is illegal and punishable by law. Please purchase only authorized electronic editions, and do not participate in or encourage electronic piracy of copyrighted materials. Your support of the author's and publisher's rights is appreciated. Karma, it's everywhere.

To Anna and Julia

An Editor's Note

The Battle of Grunwald is also known as the battle of Žalgiris (Lithuanian) or Tannenberg (German) cannot be underestimated for the effect it had on European history. It was one of the largest battles of the late-mediaeval or early modern period (estimates are between 27,000 and 66,000 total combatants) and the outcome had a long-lasting effect on the kingdoms involved. The embryonic Polish-Lithuanian state stood against the Teutonic Order and its guest knights to determine which state would survive and prosper and which would decline in importance.

The Polish and Lithuanian lands had been at odds with the Teutonic Order for over a hundred years. Although one of the Polish Dukes had invited to Order to help fight pagan forces, the Order quickly outgrew its initial reason for being there; attempting to consolidate to establish their own nation-state.

The Order sought to break up the embryonic Polish-Lithuania state that had been joined together under Jagiełło, expand their realm, and overrun the borders of these nations. The Poles and Lithuanians sought to recover parts of their native lands that the Order had conquered since their entry into Prussia.

To the surprise of European nobles, the Polish and Lithuanian forces defeated the Order's knights and killed many of their leaders in the course of the fight. While the battle did not end Teutonic Power, it helped to begin the decline of the Teutonic State that would eventually reduce it to vassal status and lead to the secularization of Prussia in 1525 under Duke Albert Hohenzollern.

The victory at Grunwald helped to secure the political and military union of Poland-Lithuania and set it on a course to be one of the largest and more powerful nations in the early-modern period. During the period of partitioned Poland in the nineteenth century, it was viewed as one of the golden moments of the kingdom and celebrated by artists like Jan Matejko. With the raise of German nationalism of the 19th century, the battle was viewed by German historians as a national disaster, so that when Field Mashal von Hindenburg defeated the Russian armies at the start of World War I, he named it the Second battle of Tannenberg in order to avenge the defeat of the Teutonic Knights.

Vincent W. Rospond

Banners of the Brothers of the Hospital of the Most Holy Mary of the Germans in Jerusalem

15th July 1410

July 15, 1410

On Tuesday, on the Day of the Messengers of the Apostles, one of the largest battles of medieval Europe was fought on the fields of Grunwald. The armies of two powerful countries clashed there: troops of the Order of the Blessed Virgin Mary of the German House in Jerusalem and numerous banners of the union of the Kingdom of Poland and the Grand Duchy of Lithuania. Today the task to determine the size of the troops that fought that day is impossible. Historians only provide an estimate the size of the royal army at 15-35 thousand men gathered in 51 Polish and 40 Lithuanian-Tatar banners. The Order's force raised and deployed in the great battle is estimated between 11,000 to 25,000 armed men composed of brother-knights, burghers and vassals living in the towns and territories of the Order's state, knightly guests and external mercenaries hired for money.

The basic combat unit of the cavalry armies of this period was the knightly Lance, usually consisting of a lance-carrying knight, a squire and one to three light-armed retainers, usually armed with crossbows, and extra remounts. However, in the Teutonic army the lance led by a brother-knight could comprise of as many as eight combatants. A certain number of knights leading their lance units was organized in larger unit, called a banner. The banner could count from several dozen to several hundred knights, men-at-arms, and retainers.

The Teutonic army at Grunwald was organized in 51 banners raised by individual commanderies, cities and towns, bishoprics as well as comprised of mercenary troops hired for money. Each banner had their own heraldic emblem on their military standards. During the medieval wars, the military flag was of great importance to the knights, members of the particular unit. Around the military standard, individual lance units gathered, orders were issued by waving of banners when in a crowded melee full of combatants, and in the event of victory, the standards were a special trophy!

After the „great slaughter", as the battle was later called by the Teutonic chroniclers, all of the Order's banners fell into Polish-Lithuanian hands, and then, as symbols of the royal triumph, they were brought in and ceremonially hung in the chapel of St. Stanislaus in the Wawel

Cathedral in Krakow in 1411 or so.

These Teutonic flags did not survive themselves but the precise images of each individual flag have been preserved and described. Conflict chronicler Jan Długosz in his most important work „Annales seu cronicae incliti Regni Poloniae" („Annals, or Chronicles of the famous Kingdom of Poland") included the descriptions of the captured banners, but in this instance even more important is the illustrated manuscript book entitled „Banderia Prutenorum", which created in 1448, was inspired by the chronicler himself and accompanied by his own commentary to the illustrations. On 48 parchment pages, Stanisław Durink a painter from Krakow, illustrated the Teutonic captured banners from Grunwald, as well as the trophies added later from the battles of Koronowo and Dąbki.

„Banderia" was this extremely original work, but unfortunately its authors did not manage to avoid making significant mistakes. Banderia was created several decades after the battle and after such a long time it was certainly not easy to link or associate the individual flags with the proper owners. Researchers know for certain that when describing the banners, Długosz used the opinion of the Order's envoys staying in Krakow in 1447 and 1448, and yet many of his entries are still controversial even today. Another issue puzzling researchers is the number of significant differences in the presentation of some banners in „Annales" written in the years 1455-1480 and „Banderia Prutenorum." In both manuscripts, the author often gave other colors, arrangements, as well as the affiliation of individual emblems, commanders or participants in the battle. Nevertheless, both books are of invaluable importance for learning about the culture and, above all, the military history of the era.

The second, no less important issue, although rarely discussed, is the number of captured banners. We know for sure that there were 52 banners in the Order's Army during the Great War, one of which, commanded by the commander from Świecie, Heinrich von Plauen, did not take part in the great battle. It is almost certain that after the victory, king Władysław II Jagiełło and duke Vitoldus had to share the spoils of war, including the particularly valuable enemy banners. According to researchers the Lithuanians took with them ten or so of captured Teutonic flags, which were later hung in the Cathedral of St. Stanislaus in Vilnius. Today it is impossible to decipher what and how many of these banners there were taken by the Lithuanian side. Among them there could have been also a number of monastic banners of lesser importance, known to have been used in the Teutonic Army, or personal banners of numerous knightly guests of the Order. The captured Teutonic banners taken by the Lithuanian side were probably burned in the great fire of the Wilno cathedral in 1530, while those kept at Wawel were observed a century after but eventually were lost in the turmoil of history, although there are reports that the remains of some were still seen in the mid- 17th century.

Banderium magistri cruciferorum maius quod magister generalis Ulricus de Junigen ducebat, in quo erant sui prestanciores curienses et milites. Paludamentum autem suum, in quo occisus est, ex albo harassio, insigni infra scripto intextum, habet ecclesia parochialis in Kije pro una casula.

Greater banner of the Teutonic Grand Master which the Grand Master Ulrich von Junigen led; in which were his most distinguished courtiers and knights. The surcoat in which he was killed, was made of fine white cloth from Arras, with the same woven sign, is kept as a chasuble in the parochial church of Kije.

One of the two main banners of the Order, under which the most eminent Teutonic knights fought, led by the Grand Master Ulrich von Jungingen himself, was a gonfanon, i.e. a type of war flag where the device of the banner was placed perpendicular to the shaft. It was made of silk and gold in 1409. The device of the banner consisted of a crowned black eagle set in the middle of the so-called crux commissa, a cross with its arms ending with straight beams. According to legend, Emperor Frederick II gave the crowned eagle to the Grand Master Herman von Salza in the 13th century. The same heraldic device was woven into the wappenrock or surcoat, the outer garment, the Grand Master wore over his armor until his death. The church in Kije, Sandomierz District, received this rich Arras cloth garment, probably as a gift from the Polish king, where it was made, after repairs and modifications, into a chasuble.

Banderium magistri cruciferorum minus sub quo erant milites cruciferorum ordinis magis notabiles et prestantes et aliqui milites mercenarii, qui ex variis Almani partibus advenerant, et aliqui curienses atque cubicularii magistri.

The lesser banner of the Order was also a gonfanon, albeit smaller than the great flag, it is device was identical with the great battle flag. This important banner, according to the chronicler Jan Długosz, fulfilled a role similar to that of a 'goncza' (renn-banner) banner in the Polish armies, and contained, apart from the better knights of the Order, also the hired knights from various parts of the Holy Roman Empire and the West as well as courtiers and chamberlains of the Grand Master.

The two main tasks of 'goncza' banner, according to various historians, were to act a as the vanguard of the army while on the march, and when in battle to open the fight with jousting, duels and skirmishes in front of the army, for the knights serving in the goncza banner ranks started the mounted armed clashes, being a series of individual knightly duels and jousting-like encounters against their opponents with battle lances and spears. These are only assumptions, as no precise descriptions of the tasks assigned to the goncza banners have survived.

Banderium ordinis cruciferorum, quod Fridericus Vallerod, magnus marsalcus Prussia ducebat nacione Francus et nobilitate insignis, qui pro armis cum sua familia defert fluvium cruce signatum et in galea gallum cristatum; qui in eodem prelio fuit occisus et in Mariemburk reductus; patruus germanus Christoferi episcopi Lubuchensis; sub quo erant milites de Franconia.

'The banner of the Teutonic Order, which was led by the Grand Marshal of Prussia, Frederick Wallerod, a native of Franconia and of noble origin, who with his family has a coat of arms a river marked with a cross and a crested rooster on helmet. He was killed in this battle and taken to Malbork. He was the uncle of brother Krzysztof, Bishop of Diocese of Lubusz, in this banner there were knights from Franconia

The third of the three main banners of the Order, commanded by the Grand Marshal of Prussia Frederich von Wallenrode who was at the same time the Commander of Königsberg, and who probably commanded the left wing of the Order's army at the battle. Apart from many excellent Teutonic knights, the knights from Franconia, like the commander, also fought under it. It was, among others, this banner that had to be on the left wing of the Order's army, because this banner clashed with and defeated the Lithuanian army in the first phase of the battle, and after their defeat, prusued them away from the main battlefield. Returning, the banners of the left wing again took part in the main fight, during which they were finally defeated and broken. Grand Marshal Fryderich von Wallenrode fell at Grunwald, and after his corpse was found on the battlefield, then together with the body of the Gand Master, they were transported to Malbork on the order of the Polish king.

Banderium Cunradi Albi, ducis Oleschniczensis Zlesie, quod presencialiter ipsemet Cunradus dux de gentibus propriis ducebat; su quo erant milites sui proprii de ducatu Vratislauiensi et de Silesia. Et ipse dux Cunradus fuit captus, et tam banderio quam omnibus fortunis suis spoliatus (...).

The banner of Konrad the White, Duke of Oleśnica from Silesia, which was personally led by Prince Konrad himself with his own people; his own knights from the Duchy of Wrocław and Silesia served under it. And Prince Konrad himself was captured and deprived of both his banner and his entire fortune (...).

Konrad VII the White is one of the two Polish nobles who supported the Teutonic Order with their banners in the Battle of Grunwald. The prince stayed for a long time at the court of Jagiełło's wife Anna Cylejska, from where he went to the Teutonic Knights to continue his education in their knightly training. At the outbreak of war, probably against his father's will, he sided with the Order, claiming that honor would not allow him to leave the Grand Master at such a time. Długosz says that during the battle Konrad was taken prisoner by a Czech knight Jost from Solec. After his release, Konrad commenced hostile actions against the Teutonic Knights and in 1414 he sparticipated as an ally of the Kingdom of Poland in battle in the so-called „Hunger War", personally taking part in the campaign alongside the Polish king.

Banderium Sancti Georgia in parte cruciferica, quod miles strenuous et qui turpe putavit ex prelio fugere, Georgius Kerzdorff ducebat. Stetit enim intrepidus tenens illudo, donec per Polonorum milites fuit captus et vexillum sibi fuit ereptum. Sub hoc errant milites insignes ex variis nacionibus terrarum Almanie satis animosi et pugnaces; et omnia fere occisi, pauci per fugam salvati (...).

Banner of St. George on the Teutonic side, which was led by a brave knight, who considered it a disgrace to flee from the battle, George Kerzdorff. He stood fearless, wielding it, until he was captured by Polish knights and his banner was torn from him. Under it were outstanding knights from various lands and German lands, very brave and valiant, and almost all of them were killed, only a few managed to escape (...).

This is one of the more controversial banners of the order. Historians to this day argue about the true identity of this flag and its commander. Długosz says that German knights fought under it and one can speculate whether they were guests or mercenaries. In „Annales" the opposite colors of this banner are given, a red cross on a white field, which opens the door to numerous polemics and questions about its true origin. There are theories that it could have been a sign one of the commanderies and even Swiss mercenary units. The same applies to the character of the commander. In 1410, among the knights in the service of the order, there were several named Gersdorff, but none was named George. It is assumed that this banner was carried at Grunwald by Christopher von Gersdorff, an envoy of Emperor Zygmunt, who was taken prisoner by the Polish knight Przedpełk Kopidłowski of the Dryja coat of arms. This unit's participation in heavy fighting may be evidenced by the fact that together with the commander, only 40 knights surrendered from a unit certainly counting several hundred warriors before the battle.

Banderium civitatis Culmensis, quod ferebat Nicolaus dictus Niksz, nacione Swewus, vexillifer Culmensis, quem magister Prussie postea, quasi parum fideliter egisset, capite dampnavit; cuius ductores erant Janussius Orzechowsky et Cunradus de Ropkow milites.

The banner of the city of Kulm (Chełmno), which was carried by Nicolaus called Niksz, a Swabian native, the Chełmno standard-bearer, whom the Prussian master later punished by cutting his throat, for allegedly not having acted faithfully. This banner was led by the knights Janusz Orzechowski and Konrad of Rapkow (from Robaków).

Nicolaus Niksz is identified with Mikołaj Ryński, a Polish knight of the Rogala coat of arms who settled in the lands around Chełmno. He was one of the founders of the Lizard Society, a knightly brotherhood, which was officially supposed to protect the nobility from the Chełmno against the lawlessness that was often committed by the local Teutonic authorities. Due to feudal duties, he took part in several war expeditions organized by the Order and for the same reasons, he found himself in the ranks of the Teutonic army at Grunwald. At the critical moment of the battle, Mikołaj Ryński lowered or abandoned the banner, signaling the Chełmno knights to retreat and stop fighting. A year later, during the reign of the new master of the Order, Henryk von Plauen, the action of the Chełmno knights was considered treason and one of the reasons for the defeat of the order in the great battle. In May 1411, on the market square in Grudziądz, the standard-bearer of Chełmno was beheaded in breach of safe conduct letter granted to Rynski from von Plauen and the general terms of the 1st Peace of Thorn.

Banderium crucifericum, quod Thomas Moerheym, thezaurarius ordinis, ducebat, qui in eodem prelio fuit occisus, et cum militibus mercenariis et familiaribus propriis satis multis, quos sub signo sui officii ducebat.

The Teutonic banner, led by Thomas Moerheym, who was the treasurer of the Order. In this battle he was killed along with a great many mercenary knights and his own servants, whom he led under the sign of his office.

Thomas von Merheim was one of the five most important Teutonic officials. As the Grand Treasurer of the order, from 1407 he was responsible for accounting and the state treasury. Usually, the Treasurer resided at the Malbork Castle and was in charge of the treasury, which was accessed by two pairs of heavy doors. Three different keys were needed to open them. The treasury could only be opened in the presence of the Treasurer, the Grand Commander and the Grand Master. The Grand Treasurer, like most of the order's dignitaries and 203 brother-knights out of about 250 monks fighting in the great battle, died on the fields of Grunwald in unknown circumstances.

Banderium episcopi Pomezaniensis, quod ducebat Marquardus de Reszemborg, sub quo erant milites terrigene de episcopatu Pomezaniensi et alii milites mercede per episcopum Pomezaniensem conducti (...).

The banner of the Pomesanian Bishop led by Marquard von Reszemburg; under it were landowners from the Pomesanian Bishopric and other mercenary knights hired for by the Pomesanian bishop (...).

The Bishop of Pomesania at that time was Johann Reyman, who, as an ally of the Order, had the banner organized consisting of knights from his bishopric and hired knights paid from the bishop's treasury. Marquard von Riesenburg, who commanded the unit, was most likely the mayor or vice-commander in one of the monastic castles in the bishopric. According to Długosz, after the battle, King Władysław sent his valet, Mikołaj Morawiec of Kunoszówka, Powala coat of arms, to Kraków with letters announcing the great victory to Queen Anne and Mikołaj Kurowski, Archbishop of Gniezno, who was ruling in the king's place during the expedition, and to the lords and burghers of Kraków. As a telling sign of this victory, the messenger took this very banner with him.

Banderium comendarie et civitas Grudzancz, quod Vilhelmus Elffenstein ducebat, sub quo erant militares et cives circumcirca et al Grudzancz habentes domicilia, quorum maior pars erat de armis, qui portant caput zubronis pro insigni: et ideo tale vexilium eis fuit consignatum (...) Comendator etiam ipse Vilhelmus Elffenstein in eodem prelio fuit occisus et plures notabiles milites proprii et mercenari cum eo.

The banner of the commandery and the city of Grudziądz, led by Wilhelm von Ellfenstein, commander of Grudziądz [Gaudenz]; under it were the knights and townspeople of the settlements around Grudziądz, most of whom were of the coat of arms of those who have a bison's head as an emblem and that is why they were given such a pennant (...). Commander Wilhelm v. Ellfenstein was killed in the battle along with a significant number of his own knights.

Wilhelm von Helfenstein, who came from Rhineland, had been a commander in Grudziądz since 1404. Previously, he performed numerous functions in the religious administration, he often took part in negotiations and agreements with Grand Duke Vitoldus. After the death of Grand Master Konrad von Wallenrode in 1393, he ruled the entire Teutonic state as an interim governor until the elections of the new Grand Master. The chronicler's note about the head of a bison in the local knights' coats of arms from the vicinity of Grudziądz was either a mistake or his invention, because nothing is known about such an emblem in the 14th and 15th centuries. Commander Helfenstein fell in battle along with most of the banner's soldiers he commanded.

Banderium comendarie et civitatis Balga, quod ducebat comendator de Balga; sub quo erant fratres militares de ordine et aliqui propria et aliqui mercenari milites.

The banner of the commandery and the city of Balga led by the commander of Balga; under it were Order's knightly brothers and some local knights, as well as hired knights.

From 1250, Balga had been the seat of the commandry in the so-called Lower Prussia, which stretched to the south-east, reaching Pisz and Elk. The Teutonic castle, the seat of the local convent, was built on the ruins of the Prussian fortress of Honeda. In 1410, Count Fryderyk von Zollern was the commander of Balga and he led the banner under his commande, although Dlugosz wrongly calls him the commander of the banner of the city of Ragnety. In 1409, after the outbreak of war with Poland, von Zollern together with Brandenburg's commander Markward von Salzbach invaded Mazovia. Balga's banner fell into the hands of Polish knights, while its commander survived the battle by fleeing the battlefield. His name later appears several times in the chronicles of the monks. He died around 1416 in Engelsberg, serving as the local commander.

Banderium comendarie et civitatis Schonsze, quod Niklosch Exclude, comendator in Schonsze, ducebat, alias Kowalyewo; sub quo errant et fratres de ordinr militares et aliqui mercenari et proprii milites.

The banner of the commander and the town of Schonsze (Kowalewo), led by Niklosz Wylcz, commander in Schonsze (Kowalewo); under it were the knightly monks and other mercenaries as well as their own knights.

The Teutonic castle in Kowalewo was erected in 1231 as a wooden and earth construction. Burnt down by Skomand of the Yotvingians, it was rebuilt, expanded and gradually strengthened, becoming the seat of the command and an important fortification in the area. According to the census carried out in 1399, the castle armory contained 56 helmets, 39 pieces of armor of various types, 10 chainmail hoods, 51 crossbows and 9,000 bolts, as well as 3 stone and lead cannons. There were a total of 81 horses in the stables, including 4 very expensive war destiers, 7 retainer horses and 12 cart horses to service the wagon train. In the farms around the castle, 2,111 pigs, 1,250 sheep and 224 cattle were bred. In 1410, the commander of Kowalewo was Nicolaus von Viltz, who died in a great battle.

Bandarium civitatis Kinszbergensis, quod ducebat vicemarsalkus seu vice-comendator Kinszbergensis (...), subquo erant etiam aliqui fratres de ordine militares et aliqui proprii, aliqui pecio conducti. Insigne autem vexilli datum civitate fuit, leo videlicet albus, per Johann, Bohemie regem, tunc in Prussia miliciam agenda in barbaros.

The banner of the city of Königsberg, was carried by the Vice-Marshal or Vice-Commander of Königsberg; under it were some knightly monks and some of their own, as well as hired knights. The emblem of the pennant, namely a white lion, was given to the city by John, the Czech king, during his expedition against the barbarians.

The city of Königsberg was founded in 1255 by the Teutonic Knights (on the site of the Prussian settlement of Tuwangste) in honor of the Czech King Premysl Otakar II, who led the Teutonic army during their next expedition against Prussia. The Teutonic Knights built a castle here, and in 1256 it was named Królewska Góra (King's Mountain). Over time, the Königsberg castle became the seat of the Königsberg commander, who also held the office of marshal of the order. The emblem of Königsberg, according to medieval records, was supposed to come from the sign of the Czech King John, who in 1329 helped the Teutonic Knights in taking over Samogitia. The Deputy Marshal in the Teutonic army is a middle-level official who took care of the smithy, saddlery and horse equipment during military expeditions. TAt Grunwald the Königsberg Banner was perhaps commanded by deputy-commander Hanus von Heydeck, who at that time held the function of a House Commander or Deputy-Commander. His fate after the battle is unknown.

𝔅anderium comendarie de Antiquo Castro, quod ducebat Wilhelmus Nyppem, Comendator de Antiquo Castro; sub que errant pauci de ordine fratres et proprii milites, sed omnes fere mercenari.

The banner of the Starogród contigient led by Wilhelm Nyppem, the Starogród commander; beneath it were a handful of brother monks and their own knights, and above all mercenaries.

Starogród (Althaus) is one of the oldest Teutonic settlements with a castle from the 13th century. The commander who led the Starogród banner near Grunwald was Eberhard von Ippenburg (Nippenburg). He died in battle.

Banderium episcopi et episcopatus Zambiensis, quod ducebat Henricus comes de Kamyenecz de Mischna; sub quo erant milites omagiales episcopatus Zambiensis et aliqui curienses episcopales et milites mercenarii per ipsum episcopum Zambiensem conducti.

The banner of the bishop and of the Sambian Bishopric that was led by Count Henry von Kamenz in Meisen; under it were the fief knights of the Sambia bishop and some of the bishop's courtiers and mercenary knights hired by the Sambia Bishop.

Długosz attributes the white banner with three red miters to the Sambia Bishop, but today it is known that this is most certainly a mistake of the chronicler. The Bishop of Sambia at that time was Heinrich von Seefeld. This emblem is not a sign of this bishopric. It looked like the banner of the Chełmno bishopric - a crossed crosier with a sword. The image of this banner is identical with the image of the commander and the city of Ragnita and it could have been the second Ragnita banner. The chronicler probably also made a mistake, designating the commander of this banner with the title of count. Heinrich von Kamenz did not come from a family of counts.

Banderium comendarie et civitatis Thucholya, quod unus ex ordine Henricus, comedator de Thucholya, ducebat; sub quo erant et fratres ordinis militares et armigeri districtus Thucholoviensis et milites mercenary (...).

The banner of the commander and the city of Tuchola, which was led by one of the Order, Hienrich, the commander of Tuchola; under it were the warrior monks and squires of the Tuchola district and mercenary knights (...).

The commander of Tuchola, Heinrich von Schwelborn, came from Franconia. In 1409, together with the commander of Człuchów, Gamrat von Pinzenau, he took part in the attack on Krajna and the capture of Bydgoszcz. According to the chronicler, from the beginning of the war, the commander ordered to have two swords carried behind him and proclaimed that he would not sheath them sooner than both would be covered in Polish blood. These displays of von Schwelborn's excessive pride seemed to have often been rebuked even by the Grand Master. In the final phase of the great battle, the commander of Tuchola abandoned his banner and shamefully ran away but was overtaken by some Polish knights in the village of Wyelhnyow (perhaps Falknowo) where he was promptly beheaded. Thus, he was punished for his pride and insolence.

Banderium magne comendarie de Sthvm, quod ducebat magne reputacionis vir, frater Cunradus Lichtersten, magnus comendator, sub quo erant de Austria milites mercenari fere omnes et pauci fratres de ordine.

The banner of the Grand Commander from Sztum was led by a great knight, Brother Conrad Lichtersten, a great commander, under which there were mostly mercenary knights from Austria and a few monk knights.

The Sztum banner had the same arrangement of colors as the Austrian one, and perhaps this was the reason why large numbers of Austrian knights gathered under it. The emblem of the Commander and the city of Sztum was carried in the battle by Heinrich von Potendorf, the Commander of Sztum, who probably survived the slaughter. In the fields of Grunwald this banner was commanded by the Grand Commander Konrad (Kuno) von Lichtenstein. During peace, he managed arsenals, ammunition production, grain warehouses, and during war he organized the army. At that time Liechtenstein was one of the closest advisors to the Grand Master. Not having his own banner, and being of Austrian descent, he probably received this banner, at the same time commanding the right wing of the Teutonic army. Konrad von Liechtenstein fell in battle, and his body, on the order of the king, together with the corpse of the Grand Master, Grand Marshal and others, was transported to Malbork and eventually buried there.

Banderium magne comendarie Nyeschoviensis, quod ducebat Gothfridus Hoczfelth, comedator of Nyeschoviensis; sub quo erant fratres de ordine et milites mercenarii.

The banner of the commander of Nieszawa, which was led by Gottfried Hatzfeld, the commander of Nieszawa, under which were warrior monks and mercenary knights.

In 1230, Konrad I of Mazowia gifted the Nieszawa stronghold to the Teutonic brothers, who built a castle there and established the southernmost Order's commandery. It was here that the truce was signed after the war of 1410. The Nieszawa commander Gottfried von Hatzfeld died at Grunwald.

Banderium militarium et stipendariorum de Vestfalia quod ducebat miles Vestfalus... Et hi proprio ere propriisque sumptibus magistro et ordini venerant in solacium, et ideo voluerunt habere proprium et domus ac generis eorum vexillum.

Banner of knights and mercenaries from Westphalia led by a Westphalian knight.

They came to help the Master and the Order with their own money and at their own expense, and therefore they wanted to have their own banner of their house and family. The Teutonic army included numerous mercenary knights and guests from many bailiwicks, monastic estates from all over Europe, especially from German lands. The banner emblem is not the emblem of Westphalia, so it may simply be a battle badge assigned to foreign knights. The banner commander is unknown.

Banderium advocacie et civitatis Rogoszno, quod frater unus ex ordine voyth Fridericus de Wed, advocatus in Rogoszno, ducebat, sub quo erant districtus Rogosznensis milites de domo et familia Doliva; in quorum decus et honorem advocacia Rogosnensis tali fuit signo insignita.

The flag of the Bailiwick and the city of Rogoźno, led by one religious brother, the Bailiff Frederick von Weden from Rogoźno; under it were knights from the Rogozno district from the house and family of Doliwa, to the glory and honor of which the Rogozno bailiwick bore such a sign.

Rogoźno (Roggenhausen) was not a town, but only a small village with a castle in the Grudziądz commandery. Since 1407 Friedrich von Wenden, who died at Grunwald, was the bailiff of Rogoźno. According to Długosz, mainly Poles, vassals of the Order living in that district, fought under the Rogozno banner, but today some researchers claim that the Doliwa coat of arms differs slightly from the emblem on the banner, and in the 14th and 15th centuries there were no nobility with this coat of arms in this area, although in in other regions of the Order´s state, these coats of arms were present.

Banderium civitatis Elbingensis et comendarie, quod ducebat Elbingensis Wernerus von Thetinger; sub quo erant militares et cives districtus et civitatis Elbingensis et aliqui fratres de ordine aliqui mercenaria.

The banner of the city of Elbląg and the commandery led by the commander of Elbląg Werner von Thetinger; under it were knights and townspeople of the district and city of Elbląg, as well as some warrior monks and some mercenaries.

One of the three banners issued by the commandery and the city of Elbing (Elbląg). In 1237, the Teutonic Knights under the command of Hermann von Balk built a small wooden and earth stronghold at the mouth of the Ilfing River, and later founded a settlement, bringing in colonists and from there they led expeditions against the pagan Prusai. The Teutonic castle was considered the most powerful and beautiful monastic castle after the castle in Malbork. Until 1309, it served as the administrative center of the Teutonic state and was the meeting place of the Prussian chapter. At Grunwald the Elbląg banner was under the command of Werner von Tettingen, a great Hospitaller, the only religious dignitary who survived the battle by escaping from the battlefield. Initially, he found shelter in the Elbląg Castle, from where he was chased away by the townspeople. Then he reached Malbork, where his health deteriorated, and he died in 1413.

Banderium comendarie et civitatis Engelszberk, quod ducebat Byrkardus Wobek, comedator in Engelszberk, que in Polonico Koprivwno apellatur; sub quo militabant fratres de ordine et nonnulli stipendarii precio condycti.

The banner of the commandery and the city of Engelsburg (Pokrzywno), led by Burkard Wobek, commander of Engelsberg, which in Polish is called Koprzywno; under it fought Order brother-knights and some hired knights.

Engelsberg Castle was built in the 13th century, and although the commander's seat was located there, this stronghold was never great. Most often it performed the administrative and provisioning functions for the Order's army. Tons of grain, huge amounts of fish, meat, cheese and salt were stored in its granaries, stores and pantries. Cattle and horses, including some combat ones, were bred in this commandery. In 1410, the commander post was held by Burchard von Wobecke, who had earlier held much more important offices in the Order — Treasurer of the Order (1397-1404) and Grand Clothier (1404-March 1410), high offiial managing and organizing Order's clothing and armor. It is not known why Wobecke became commander in Engelsberg. At Grunwald, he led the banner of his commandery, and died in battle.

Banderium comendarie et civitatis Brodniczensis, quod ducebat Bayjdemin Stoll, comedator Brodniczensis alas Stroszberk; sub quo Erant et fratres de ordine et milites districtus Brodniczensis et aliqui milites mercenaria.

The banner of the commandery and the city of Brodnica, led by Baldwin Stoll, commander of Brodnica, i.e. Strassburg; under it were the monks and knights of the Brodnica district and some mercenary knights.

Baldwin Stoll (Stal, Stael, Stahel) in the years 1402-1408 was the Bailiff of the New March, and from December 1409 he was appointed commander in Brodnica. The castle and the developing urban center were located on an important trade route connecting the lands of Chełmno with Mazovia. Until the 13th century, a wooden and earth watchtower of the Mazovian princes stood in this place. After Konrad I of Mazovia brought the Teutonic Knights to Poland and the Order forged the document of the duke granting them the land of Chełmno and other the conquests in Prussia into perpetual possession, the monks also occupied Brodnica and began to build a brick fortress in stead of the old stronghold. Between 1335 and 1337, a Teutonic commandery was established in Brodnica. Baldwin Stoll fell at Grunwald.

Banderium episcopatus et episcopi Chelmensis, quod curiensis episcopalis Theodoricus de Sowemborg ducebat, sub quo erant et familiares atque curienses et omagiales terrigene...episcopi Chelmensis, qui pro ea tempestate sedem Chelmensem regebat.

The banner of the bishopric and the bishop of Chełmno led by the bishop's courtier Teodoric von Sowemburg; under it were householders, courtiers, and vassal knights... of the Bishop of Chełmno, who at that time ruled the capital of Chełmno.

It seems that Długosz in „Banderia Prutenorum" most likely confuses the sign of the Chełmno bishopric with the signs of the Sambia bishopric. He also makes similar mistakes in his chronicle. Knights from the Chełmno bishopric could fight in the Chełmno or German banners, or under signs that are impossible to recreate today. The Sambian bishop in 1410 was Henryk von Seefeld, and the Chełmno bishop was Arnold Stapel. The last one was a member of the Teutonic Order and even served as Chancellor of the Grand Master. The commander of the bishop's army at Grunwald could have been Theodoric von Sonnenburg.

Banderium advocacie castri Brathian et Nove Civitatis, quod Johannes de Redere, advocatus de Brathian, ducebat; sub quo erant aliqui milites de ordine et aliqui cives Nove civitatis et precio conducti stipendarii.

The banner of the mayor of the Bratian castle and the New Town led by Johann von Redere, the mayor of Bratian, under which were some knights and some townspeople from Nowe Miasto and mercenaries.

The castle in Bratian was built in the first half of the 14th century, probably by the Teutonic Knights of Swiss origin. In 1343 or 1359, the seat of the religious Bailiff from Nowe Miasto (Neumarkt) was moved to it. It was in its vicinity that on July 10-12, 1410, when the Polish army declined to cross and moved away from the fortified ford on the Drwęca River near Kurzętnik, that the Teutonic army crossed to the other bank of this river by twelve pontoon bridges and headed towards Lubawa, to finally reach the fields of Grunwald. Johann von Redere was at that time the Teutonic Bailiff in Bratian and rather died in battle, because from October 1410 this function was held by Heinrich Marschall.

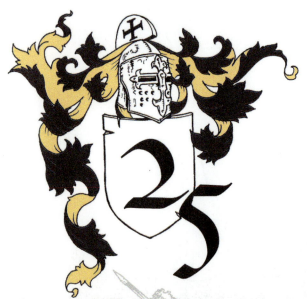

Banderium civitatis Brunsberg (...); sub quo erant terrigene et omagiales et cives districtus Brunsbergensis et aliqui milites mercede conducti.

Banner of the city of Brunsberg (Braniewo)(...); under it were the landowners and vassals as well as the burghers of the Brunsberg district and other mercenary knights.

Braniewo was the oldest town in Warmia oned by Bishops of Warmia. The first settlement, founded in 1240, was repeatedly destroyed in Prussian uprisings and was rebuilt after 1250, and in 1254 it received city rights. During the Second Prussian uprising, the city had been refounded, it was destroyed and again rebuilt in 1274. At the same time, a brick castle was erected, which became the first seat of the Warmian bishops. In the 13th century, the town became an important trade center and the only Warmian seaport. Since 358 it had been a member of the Hanseatic League, a confederation of Northern and Central European guilds, cities and towns intended to facilitate and defend commercial trade among them. Presumably, the two crosses on the flag refer to this relationship, but it may also be religious symbolism.

Banderium militum Almanorum (...); sub quo erant Theutunites milites de..., qui propriis impensis pro ordine militabant et propria generis proprieque domus et familie ferebant vexilum.

Banner of German knights(...); under it were German knights who fought for the Order at their own expense and carried the banner of their own family, home and family.

Długosz claimed that it was a banner composed of guests of the Order, because they fought, unlike the mercenaries, „at their own expense". Perhaps they were German knights, although there is no more precise information about where they came from and what their number was. Their commander's identity also remains unknown. Due to the similarity of the sign to the banner of Gniew, some historians conclude that it could have been the second banner of Gniew. It is certain that in the great battle the Order army was aided and supported, apart from the mercenaries, by the so-called guests of the Order. Długosz mentioned at least a dozen or so nations fighting on the side of the Order: Poles, Livonians, Czechs, Moravians, Silesians, Bavarians, Meisenians, Austrians, Rhinelanders, Swabians, Frisians, Lusatians, Thuringians, Pomeranians, Stettinians, Kashubians, Saxons, Franconians, Westphalians and Prussian knights.

Banderium gentis et nacionis Sweyczerorum, qui propriis sumptibus magistro et ordini tulerant subsidium (...). Et idea sue nacionis sueque regionis et gentis deferabant pro signo vexilium.

The banner of the tribe and nation of the Swiss who, at their own expense, helped the master and the order (...). And that's why they had the sign of their nation and their area on the banner.

Like several other banners in Długosz´s descriptions, this also raises numerous controversies, as does the participation of the Swiss in the great battle. The banner did not represent the sign of any Swiss land, which, however, did not determine their participation or lack thereof in the Teutonic army. The banner emblem was similar to the coat of arms of the von Fischborn family from Franconia, which was strongly associated with the Order. The representative of the family could have been an ensign or commander of this unit. However, there is a theory that it could have been the second banner of the Balga commandery, due to the similarity of the sign.

Banderium secundum civitatis et comendarie de Elbingo, quod ducebat vicecomendator Elbingensis, subquo erant fratres de ordine militareset terrigene districtus Elbingensis et milites stipendium merentes.

The second banner of the city and commandery of Elbląg, which was led by the vice-commander of Elbląg; under it were the knights and landowners of the Elbląg district, as well as knights serving for pay.

The second of three banners issued by the commandry and the city of Elbląg. The commander of this expedition was the vice-commander of Elbląg Ulrich von Stoffen. His further fate is unknown. He could have followed the example of commander von Tettingen, and run away from the battlefield, but because he no longer appeared later in any documents known today, he may also have died in battle. There are records that in the war with Poland in the summer of 1410 Elbląg lost 550 people and if this is true, it probably applies to all three banners.

Banderium advocacie et civitatis Leszken, quod Henricus Kuszeczke, advocatus de Leszken, ducebat, que in Polonico vocatur Zyolawa; sub quo erant fratres de ordine militares ex castro Mariemburgensi et aliqui advocati sive sculteti opidorum et villarum de Zolava.

The banner of the mayor's office and the city of Leszken (Laski), led by Heinrich Kuszeczke, the Bailiff of Leszken, which in Polish is called Zyolawa; under it were the knights from the Malbork Castle and some mayors and village leaders from towns and villages in Żuławy.

In „Annales", Długosz attributes this banner to the town of Lasin belonging to the Bailiff in Rogoźno with the village of Laski in Żuławy. The Bailiff of the Teutonic Order managing the area of Wielkie Żuławy Malborskie (Great Zulawy of Malbork) appeared as early as 1321. The village of Laski being a Bailiwick of the Order in Żuławy was a seat for the Order's overseers for the maintenance and construction of flood embankments and was directly subordinated to their supervisor in Malbork. War horses were bred at the extensive manor, and a cavalry marshal (Pferdemarschall) also resided there. From 1407, Konrad von Kunseck (Königsegg) was the Bailiff of Laski. He died at Grunwald.

Banderium burgensium de Elbingo, quod ducebat... magister civium Elbingensis; sub quo non erant nisi cives Elbingenses et aliqui milites precio conducti a civibus Elbingensibus.

The banner of the townspeople of Elbląg led by..., the mayor of Elbląg; under it were only Elbląg townspeople and some knights hired for the money of Elbląg townspeople.

The third banner put up by Elbląg. In "Annales", Długosz wrongly attributed this banner to the knights of Meissen. At Grunwald, a banner of 216 people, including 180 horsemen, was led by the Mayor of Elbląg, Heinrich Monch. Other townspeople, known by name who took part in the battle, were Bertram Betke, Klaus Kustrat, Jan von Hervorden, Jan Raue, Henryk Altmann, Tidemann von der Wilde, and Heirich Kreuzburg. Peter Vroydenberg commanded the wagon train, and a certain Roland and a goldsmith Nicolaus commanded the banner's infantry. Mayor Monch and councilors Betke and Kustrat survived the rout of the Teutonic forces, probably fleeing the battlefield.

Banderium comendarie et civitatis Slochow, quod ducebat Arnoldus de Baden, comendator Slochoviensis, sub quo erant aliqui fratres militares de ordine et aliqui terrigene et milites et cives districtus et civitatis Slochouiensis. Occisus autem fuit prefatus Arnoldus de Baden commendator Slochouiensis, cum pluribus militibus sui vexilli, et inter cadavera occisorum repartus, in Marienburg ad sepulturam relatus.

The banner of the commandery and the city of Człuchów, led by Arnold von Baden, commander of Człuchów; under it there were some knightly monks and some landowners, knights and townspeople from the vicinity of Człuchów. The aforementioned commander Arnold von Baden, together with numerous knights from his banner, was killed and his body found among the corpses of fallen, and then transported for burial to Malbork.

The Człuchów banner is almost identical to the flag of the Warmia bishopric, it differs only in a few details. Again, the question arises whether this is another mistake of Długosz. At that time the coat of arms of the city of Człuchów looked completely different, it had bull's head on it. The next question mark when describing this banner is the character of its commander. The chronicler said that he died in battle, and his body was transported to Malbork together with the body of the Grand Master. Meanwhile, some historians state that Arnold von Baden, the commander of Człuchów from April 1410 and the companion-adjutant of the last two Grand Masters of the Order survived the battle. It is also possible that he was not present at all in the Grunwald fields. He did die in August 1410.

Banderium civitatis Bartensten, quod ducebat..., advocatus de Bartensten; sub quo erant nonnulli fratres de ordine militares et terrigene districtus Bartenstenensis, qui asciam, in Polonico oxa, in Bohemico bradacziczam, deferunt pro insigni, quam etiam tunc deferebant pro vexilli signo.

The banner of the city of Bartenstein (Bartoszyce), led by ..., the procurator of Bartenstein; under it were numerous knightly monks and landowners of the Bartenstein district, who had an axe, in Polish "oksza", in Czech "bradaczcza", as an emblem and carried such a sign on the banner.

Already in 1240, on the conquered lands of the Prussian tribe of Bartians, the Teutonic Knights built one of the oldest monastic castles. The area around it was inhabited by settlers from Hesse, Brandenburg and Masovia. Initially, this fortress was the seat of the Bailiff, later the prosecutor, a lower Order official subordinate to the commander in Balga, resided there. In the years 1390-1391, the Lithuanian prince Vitoldus stayed at the castle in Bartoszyce, at that time seeking support from the Teutonic Knights in the struggle for power in Lithuania. The image on the banner undoubtedly refers to the emblem of the city, which is represented by an ax. The commander leading the Bartoszyce banner into battle is unknown.

Banderium comendarie et civitatis Osterrodensis, quod Penchenhavn, comendator Osterrodensis, ducebat, cuius ferentarius fuit Peregrinus dictus Fogel, vexillifer Osterrodensis; sub quo erant et fratres de ordine militares et terrigene omagiales sub commendaria Osterrodensi consistens.

The banner of the commandery and the city of Osterode (Ostróda), led by the commander Ostróda Penchenhavn, and whose standard-bearer was Peregrin called Fogel, the standard-bearer of Ostróda; under it were brother-monks of the knightly status and vassal landowners subject to the Ostróda commandery.

The Teutonic castle in Osterode (Ostróda) was erected around 1300 on the important trade route from Mazovia to the Baltic Sea. The first settlers from Saxony came from the city of Osterode, and this is probably where the name of the new town and the commandery established there came from in 1341. The castle garrison was to protect the area against the growing in frequency Lithuanian raids. In August 1409 after the declaration war on the Kingdom of Poland Commander of Ostroda Gamrath (Conrad) von Pinzenau, together with Heinrich von Schwelborn the commander of Tuchola, invaded Polish Crown territory of Krajna, a border region land between Wielkopolska and Kashubia, and captured Bydgoszcz. In 1410, at Grunwald, Commander of Ostroda von Pinzenau was the banner's commander. Probably due to the fact that the great battle took place in the Ostróda commandery lands, he and his banner were at the side of the Grand Master's reserve command in the last hope attack of the Order's grand reserve in the great battle. Gamrath von Pinzenau fell at Grunwald.

Banderium comendarie et civitatis Scithno, quod comes Albertus de Eczbor, comedator in Ortelszburg idem Scithno, duxerant; sub quo erant fratres militares de ordine et terrigene omagiales ad dictam comendariam in Ortelszburg pertinentes.

The banner of the commandery and the town of Szczytno, led by count Albert von Eczbor, commander in Ortelszburg, i.e. Szczytno; under it were brother knights of the Order and vassal landowners belonging to this commandery.

The castle in Ortelsburg (Szczytno) was first built in the form of a wood-and-earth watchtower in the mid-fourteenth century, and then in the years 1370-1390 upgraded to a brick fortress that was aimed at protecting both the surrounding area and the rapidly growing settlement around the castle populated mainly by the Polish settlers from nearby Mazovia. The name most probably comes from the name of the founder of the castle, Ortulf von Trier who was the Great Hospitaller and commander of Elbląg. In 1410, there was no commandery seat at Szczytno, and the pfleger (burgrave or Bailiff) of the Order, whose name has not been preserved, presided there while the castle was a feudatory to the Commandery at Elbląg. Albert von Eczbor does not appear in any surviving Order documents.

Banderium civitatis Rangnetha et comendarie, quod ducebat comendator de Rangnetha, comes Fridericus de Czolrn; sub quo erant fratres militares de ordine et convent Ragnetesi et terrigene omagiales commendarie et regionis Ragnetensis.

The banner of the city of Ragneta and the commandry led by the commander of Ragneta, Count Fryderyk von Czolrn (Zollern); under it were the knights from the commandery of Ragneta and vassal landowners from the commandery and the surrounding area of Ragneta.

When describing this banner Jan Długosz was also wrong or received imprecise descriptions from his source. The images on the banner, sometimes described as miters and sometimes as helmets, do not differ from those described as the emblem of the Sambia bishopric. As with many it is highly probable that the Ragneta commandery deployed as many as two units. It is not known, however, who was the commander of Ragnea at that time. Count Frederick von Zollern, mentioned in the description, was then the commander of Balga, and his predecessor was Johann von Sayn, commander of Toruń was killed in the great battle. The name of the next Order official at the Ragneta castle appeared only at the end of 1410 and he was Helfrich von Drahe.

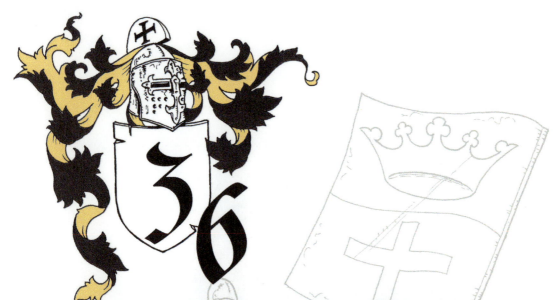

Banderium civitatis antique Kunigsperk alias Crolowgrod, quod ducebat civium magister Kunigsbergensis ex propriis civibus et terrigenis ore ipsius et ex mercenariis militibus collectum.

The banner of the Old Town of Königsberg, i.e. King's Town, led by the mayor of Königsberg, composed of its townspeople and landowners as well as mercenary knights.

In „Annales" Długosz described this banner as the emblem of Knipawa, which is an obvious mistake. Certainly, it was correctly classified in the „Banderia Prutenorum" and it was the color of one of the three banners of the Old Town of Königsberg. Old Town (Altstadt), was established in the place of the former Prussian settlement of Tuwangste in honor of the Czech king Přemysl Otakar II, who in the years 1254-1255 took part in the crusades against the Prussians. The new castle and town were called the Royal Mountain - Königsberg, over time it became the main center of Lower Prussia, and from 1312 the main seat of the Grand Marshal of the Order. The identity of the mayor of Königsberg, leading the banner at Grunwald, is unknown.

Banderium militum de Reno et de Almania, quod ducebat..., miles, sub quo locate erant sexaginta lancee de militibus egregiis et prestantibus Rinensibus et Almanicis (et) Liuonitis, ferendo ausilia cruciferis de propria substancia; et ideo proprium et singulare habuerunt banderium genus eorum, nacionem et familiam representans.

The banner of the Rhenish and German knights led by..., a knight; under it were 60 lances of the greatest and most eminent knights of the Rhineland, Germany and Livonia, who helped the Teutonic Knights at their own expense and therefore had their own and separate banner, denoting their tribe, nation and family.

In „Annales" Dlugosz gave this banner to the German and Rhenish knights, and only later added the Livonian knights. As it is written in the description, the best German knights who came to help the Order with their own money were under it. According to the chronicler there were about 60 lances fighting there, which made it at least 180 men strong. The lance was the basic fighting unit in the medieval army and usually consisted of a knight with a lance and one, two or more lighter armed retainers, armed with bow or crossbow. However, the composition of the lance could have differed depending on the wealth of the knight or his origin. The lances of the Order often consisted of nine men: a brother-knight and eight lighter-armed retainers and bowmen. The participation of Livonian knights was possible within this banner's ranks, because the Livonian Order residing in Livonia in 1237, in a way, merged that land with the Teutonic state, retaining, however, far-reaching autonomy. The expansion of the Order to the north was stopped by the prince of Novgorod, Alexander Nevsky, who defeated the Order's army on the frozen waters of Lake Peipus.

Banderium advocacie et civitatis Tczow, quod ducebat Mathias Beberach advocatus Tschoviensis; sub quo erant fratres militares de ordine et terrigene regionis illius et cives Tczczouiensis et aliqui stipendarii forenses et precio conducti.

The banner of the mayor's office and the town of Tczew led by Mathias Beberach, the Bailiff of Tczew; under it were brother knights and landowners from this area, as well as burghers and some mercenaries.

The fortified stronghold at Tczew (Dirschau) was built on the initiative of the Pomeranian Prince Sambor II and the capital of his duchy was moved there. In 1308, the Teutonic Knights seized the town by deceit and destroyed it. At the castle the new administration of the Teutonic monastic state began to rule and govern. In the years 1364-1383, the town began to develop under the Chełm law under the jurisdiction of the Order. The Bailiff of Tczew initially fell under the authority of the commander of Gdańsk, and later he fell directly under the central management of Malbork. In 1410, the Bailiff Mathias von Bebern, , who had held this office since 1402, led the Tczew banner to the Grunwald battlefield where he died in the great battle.

Banderium civitatis Holsten maioris, que in Theutunico vocatur Melzak, quod ducebat advocatus de Holsten..., sub quo erant et fratres militares de ordine Olstenenses et terrigene ac cives districtus Olstenensis et milites mercenarii.

The banner of the larger city of Olsztyn, which in German is called Melzak, led by the Bailiff of Olsztyn..., and under it there were also knightly brothers from Olsztyn, landowners and townspeople of the Olsztyn district and mercenary knights.

At that time, the two towns mentioned above were located within the Warmian Chapter: Allenstein (Olsztyn) and Melzak (Pieniężno). The chronicler wrongly identified both cities, and at the same time misrepresented the situation as if there was a Teutonic castle in Olsztyn with an incumbent Bailiff. The well-fortified castle was in fact the property of the Warmia Chapter subordinated to bishop Heinrich Heilsberg von Vogelsang. The banner could have belonged to the Bishop of Warmia.

Banderium militum Mischnensium, sub quo erant optuaginte haste militum egregiorum et virorum Misnensium, qui sub propriis impensis et armis cruciferorum ordini venerant in subsidium. Qui nolebant sub aliquo signo alieno cruciferico pugnare, sed proprii generis, familie et domus singno assumpto pugne intererant (...).

The banner of the Meissen knights, under which there were eighty lances of the greatest knights and men of Meissen, who came to the aid of the Teutonic Order at their own expense and with their own weapons and who did not want to fight under any foreign sign, but having accepted their own flag, took part in the battle (...).

Initially, this banner was identified with the mercenaries or guests from the German lands, and later a note about the knights from Meissen was added to „Banderia Prutenorum". Lupold Köckeritz von Ecber in Lusatia is depicted in the foreground of the illustration. He was not a member of the Order, but as a guest he rendered numerous services to the Teutonic Knights, for which he received generous rewards. In the Malbork cash book, he appeared as one of the best-paid knights. He was an envoy to the court of the Mazovian prince, he took part in raids on Samogitia and Lithuania, as well as on a sea raid to Gotland. It can be assumed that he significantly contributed to the enlistment of the entire banner of knights from Meissen. At Grunwald he belonged to the elite banner of the Grand Master. In the last tactical advance of the Teutonic reserve banners, he attacked the retinue of the Polish King alone and paid for his act with his life. He was knocked off his horse by the royal secretary Dobiesław of Oleśnica and was finished off at the hands of the king's bodyguards.

Banderium civitatis Brandenburgensis, quod Markwarth de Szalczbach, comendator Brandenburgensis ducebat; sub quo errant fratres militares de ordine et terrigene ac cives Brandenburgenses nonnulique milites precio conducti. Quod quidem signum et banderium per...marchionem Brandenburgensem donatum et apprivilegiatum fuit civitati Brandenburgensi, dum ipse marchio Brandenburgensis exegisset miliciam in Prussia in barbaros (...).

The banner of the city of Brandenburg (Pokarmin), led by Markward von Szalczbach, commander of Brandenburg; under it were brother-knights of the Order as well as Brandenburg landowners and townspeople and numerous mercenaries. This emblem and the banner were given as a privilege to the city of Brandenburg by ... the Margrave of Brandenburg, when he was fighting in Prussia against the barbarians (...).

Brandenburg Castle was founded in 1265 by Otto the Pious, Margrave of Brandenburg, when he was taking part in his third expedition to Prussia. Markward von Salzbach was the commander of Brandenburg from 1402. In a great battle he was taken prisoner by Jan Długosz of Niedzielsk, Wieniawa coat of arms, and together with the Land Master of Samogitia, Schönburg, and Jurga Marschalk who had been a Grand Master's companion, were handed over to Grand Duke Vitoldus who had them beheaded! Długosz explained that the reason for the prince's anger was the bold words of the Teutonic Knights. Earlier, during the congress on the Nemunas near Kaunas, both brother-knights allegedly insulted Vitoldus' mother with abusive words. There is a view among many historians that that the reason for such a quick execution was quite different. It was supposedly done to hide Vitoldus' old agreements with the Teutonic Knights, in which both knightly monks were important witnesses. Von Salzbach participated in the signing of the treaty on the Elk River between the prince and the Order, where the Order was to aid and provide support to the prince in the civil war in Lithuania in 1390, in 1399 he commanded the forces of the Order supporting Vytautas' army during the campaing and in the lost battle against the Tatars on the Worskla River.

Banderium Kazimiri ducis Stolpensis alias Stetinensis, quod presencialiter ipsemet Kazimirus dux cu sius gentibus ducebat non sine sua et nominis sui ac gentis et nacionis sue ac Kingwarii maxima ignominia et dedecore, sacra auri fame devictus, sibi et generi suo atque prosapie opprobrium inusturus sempiternum (...).

The banner of Casimir, Duke of Słupsk, or Szczecin, led personally by Prince Casimir himself of his people, not without the greatest humiliation and dishonor of his name, nation and language, possessed by a cursed lust for gold, having burnt the eternal mark of disgrace on himself, his family and his descendants (...).

Casimir V, Duke of Szczecin, was only 22 years old during the Battle of Grunwald. He went to war on the side of the Order, wanting to gain an ally against the Duchy of Brandenburg' incursions harassing his lands. Since the 14th century, the Western Pomeranian rulers frequently changed allies and alliances, once going to the Polish side, other times to the Teutonic side. From 1407, Bogusław VIII Słupski and his nephew Casimir V stood on the side of the Order. During the battle, the prince and several knights were taken prisoner by a Krakow banner knight Jakub Skarbek of Gora, Habdank clan of Sandomierz Land and handed over to the king. After the battle, king Władysław II invited him to a triumphal feast, and on June 8, 1411, he was released from captivity upon a guarantee from prince Bogusław VIII, the Duke of Stargard and Słupsk, and after paying a large ransom in Krakow on St. Martin's Day, i.e. November 11, 1410.

Banderium militarium Terre Culmensis, quod Johannes comes et heres de Seyn, comendator Thorunensis, ducebat; sub quo errant fratres de ordine et terrigene ac cives Thorunenses ac Chelmenses et milites mercenarii a civibus Thorunensibus conducti.

The banner of the knighthood of the Chełmno Land led by count Johann von Seyn, commander and heir of Toruń; under it were brother-knights, landowners and townspeople of Toruń and Chełmno, as well as mercenaries hired by Toruń burghers.

The commander's castle in Toruń, whose construction began in the 13th century, was a base during the Prussian conquests and was one of the oldest Teutonic structures on the Vistula River. Due to its frontier location, the Toruń commandery played an important administrative role within the Teutonic state, and its commanders were often the main advisers to the Grand Masters. In the great war, the townspeople of Toruń themselves fielded 214 men-at-arms. Johann von Sayn came from a well-known Holy Roman empire count family, that had rendered service and contributions to the Teutonic Order, from April 1410 he held the office of commander at the Toruń commandery. He fell in battle, and his body, together with the body of the Great Master, was sent to Malbork for burial.

Banderium comendarie et civitatis Gdanensis, quod ducebat ex propriis et mercenariis gentibus magister civium Gdanensis, terrigenis videlicet et civibus et ex nauticibus maritimisque militibus, qui vocantur schewkindri, hominibus audacibus et animosis et nullum genus mortis abhorrentibus, magis tamen pugna navali et maritima, quam terrestri calentibus; qui banderium Gdanense usque at centum hastatos compleverant et strennuorum militum de se in pugna signa ostendebant (...).

The banner of the commandery and the city of Gdańsk, led by the Bailiff of Gdańsk, made up of his own people and mercenaries, landowners, townspeople and sea sailors, whom they call „schewkindri", courageous people of great spirit, unafraid of any kind of death, but preferring to fight on ships and sea rather than on land; they completed the Gdańsk banner to the number of 100 lances and showed great courage in battle (...).

Since the beginning the 11th century, Gdańsk, thanks to its location, was an extremely important commercial and administrative center in Gdansk Pomerania. In 1308, during the invasion of the Brandenburg army, the town was taken over and the Teutonic Knights were summoned to help defend the castle with the consent of King Władysław I Łokietek. The brother-knights recaptured the town, seized the castle, and then proceeded to slaughter the inhabitants, and commenced the conquest of Gdansk Pomerania. In 1346, Gdańsk obtained the city rights under the Chełmno law, and in 1361 joined the Hanseatic League. At Grunwald, the commandery and the city of Gdańsk put up three banners, and according to records, out of 1,200 armed men, about 300 died. At that time, there were two mayors in the Gdańsk stronghold - Arnold Hecht and Konrad Letzkau, but it is not known which of them commanded the banner. Both survived the debacle, and after the battle recognized the protection of the Polish King over Gdańsk. After the withdrawal of Polish troops from the territory of the Order's state in April 1411, the new commander Heinrich von Plauen the Younger invited representatives of the city council of Gdańsk to the castle, where they were cruelly murdered.

Banderium comendarie de Gdansk, quod ducebat Johannes Schonenfhelt, comendator Gdanensis; sub quo erant fratres militares de ordine domus et conventus Gdanensis, item terrigene et militares districtus Gdanensis et milites precio conducti forenses. Banderium alterum comendarie et castri Gdansk, quod ex fratribus cruciferis et mercenariis militibus ducebat vicecomendator Gdanensis, in quo erant septuaginta haste militum nobilium.

The banner of the Gdańsk commandery led by the Gdańsk commander Jan Schönenfeld; under it were brother-knights from the house and convent of Gdańsk, as well as landowners, knights and mercenaries. The second banner of the commandery and the city of Gdańsk, composed of Teutonic brothers and mercenary knights, was led by the Vice-Commander of Gdańsk, and in which there were 70 lances of noble knights.

Two banners issued by the Gdańsk commandery. The first of them was commanded by the Commander Johann von Schönfeld himself, and the second by the vice-commander, who could have been Kunz von Westa from Meissen. The commander managed to survive the debacle at Grunwald, escaped from the battlefield, and returned to Gdańsk and, in agreement with the townspeople, organized a defense there and even sent 400 sailors to Malbork. Relations between the city and the castle quickly deteriorated, however, there were riots in which even guests of the Order and mercenaries, brought to Gdańsk after the battle due to illnesses and wounds, were murdered. The city paid homage to the king and officially joined the Polish side. After the withdrawal of the Polish army from the borders of the Order state, the conflict did not end and lasted until 1413, when the mayors were murdered through deceit. The authority was taken over again by the Teutonic Knights, but the internal cooperation and state of affairs did not return to that state that had existed before the great war.

Banderium episcopatus Warmiensis alias Elszberk civitatis, quod ducebat ... familiaris et curiensis... episcopi Warmiensis, sub quo erant et terrigene omnes in frequenti numero episcopatus Warmiensis et cives civitatis Elszberk et curienses ac familiares prefati... episcopi Warmiensis, qui centum numerum hastatorum et ultra coplebant.

The banner of the Warmian bishopric, i.e. the city of Elszberk (Lidzbark Warmiński), led by ... a householder and courtier of ... the Bishop of Warmia; under it were all the landowners of the Warmian Bishopric in great numbers and the townspeople of the city of Elszberk, as well as the courtiers and household of the Bishop of Warmia, who made up the number of over 100 lances.

The banner's insignia was very similar to the emblem of Człuchów. It is possible that the Bishop of Warmia issued two banners. The Bishop of Warmia at that time was Henryk Heilsberg von Vogelsang. The diocese was established in Prussia by the decree of the Papal Legate William of Modena on July 29, 1243. It was established in the territories occupied by the pagan Prussians, and took its name from the Prussian tribe of the Warmians. The decree of William of Modena in the same year 1243, on July 30, was approved by Pope Innocent IV. The first Bishop of Warmia was a Bishop Anselm appointed by the pope on October 6, 1250. The Diocese of Warmia was the largest diocese in the Teutonic state.

Banderium civitatis Thorunensis, quod ducebat Thorunensis magister civium, de domesticis et precio conductis gentibus, et plures milites forenses et mercenarii a Thorunensibus precio conducti, qui numerum octuaginta hastatorum explebant.

The banner of the city of Toruń, which the mayor of Toruń led from local people and people recruited for money, as well as numerous foreign and mercenary knights hired by the inhabitants of Toruń, who made up the number of eighty lances.

Eighty lances from Toruń was, according to records, a unit numbering from 214 to 240 men. It is known that they suffered heavy losses in the battle, there were many killed and captured. Descriptions of the banners of the city of Toruń in the works of Długosz show significant discrepancies. In „Annales", the chronicler indicated as their commander the Vice-Commander of commandery of Toruń, whom could have been Mikołaj Röder, who still held this office in 1407, although it is not known whether he was the one at the time of Grunwald. „Banderia Prutenorum" indicated as the commander of the banner the mayor of Toruń, Albrecht Rothe, together with the second mayor, Johannes von der Merse, which was probably more likely. Both commanders were taken prisoner and survived the war.

Banderium comendarie, castri et civitas Gnyew alias in Theytonico Mewe, quod ducebat Johannes comes de Veynde, comendator Gnyevensis, homo nobilis et manswetus, et qui semper et pro omni tempore concordiam et pacem magnopere swasit et consuluit (...).

The banner of the commandery, of the castle and the city of Gniew, in German Mewe, led by Count Johann von Veynde, commander of Gniew, a noble and gentle man who always and at all times advised harmony and peace (...).

In „Annales", Długosz stated that the Gniew banner included landowners and townspeople from this district, as well as knights who came from Franconia. The most mysterious figure is the banner commander. The chronicler described count Johann von Wende as one who always preached peace instead of war and whom Tettingen, the commander of Elbląg, suspected of cowardice and advised him to return home. „I have no doubt that I have advised well that peace is better than war," replied the Count of Wende. „And you, commander, beware lest you escape from this war a coward!" They were prophetic words. Johann von Wende was killed in the battle, and Tettingen fled the battlefield, abandoning his banner. The story would be unusual if it wasn't for the commander of the Gniew banner, who does not appear in any other document at that time. The commander in Gniew was then Segemunt von Ramungen, who also fell at Grunwald. Historians identify Count Johann von Wende with the person of the Mayor of Rogoźno, Fryderyk von Wende.

Banderium civitatis. que dicitur Swyatha Szyekirka, in Theutonico Elge-beyth, quod ducebat advocatus de Szwyantha Szyekyrka ex militibus ordiniis propriis et mercenariis collectum.

The banner of the city, which is called Saint Axe, in German Elgebeyth, Heiligenbeil, led by the mayor from Saint Axe, composed of both own and mercenary knights.

Before 1272, in the place of the later Teutonic town, there was a Prussian settlement called Swentomest (Holy Place). In 1301, near the sacred oak, a Prussian place of pagan worship, a town was founded under the Chełmno law named Heiligenstadt (Holy City), which in 1344 was changed to Heiligenbeil (hence the Polish name Święt Siekierka, although the ending „beil" may come from the Old Prussian „bil' meaning village or castle). In the Middle Ages, the name Święto Miejsce was used. In 1410, there was no Bailiff of the Order there and it is believed that it could have been the second Balgian banner led by the Balga vice--commander, although the sign is identical to the emblem of Bartenstein (Bartoszyce)

Banderium civitatis Brunszwik, quam ... dux Brunszwiczensis miliciam contra barbaros tunc agens in Prussia condiderat, et cui ex suo nomine et ducatu Brunszwik nomen indiderat armaque sua suique ducatus (....), sub que erant fratres militares de ordine et terrigene atque cives districtus et civitatis prefate Brunszwiczensis.

The banner of the city of Brunswick, which ... the Duke of Brunswick, once fighting against the barbarians in Prussia, ordered to be made, providing his name and the name of the duchy and granted the privilege of wearing the coat of arms of his duchy as an emblem (...). There were religious brothers of the knighthood, landowners and burghers of the district and city of Brunswick under it.

There was no place or commandery called Brunswick in Prussia, so it is probably a complete invention of the author. Undoubtedly, such a banner existed and today it is attributed to German guests or mercenary knights from Hesse, and even more probably from Thuringia. During the first year of the great war of 1409-1410, according to data from the Teutonic army register and pay book, the Order enlisted 5,751 mercenaries, of whom 3,712 (or, according to other data, slightly more than 4,000) took part in the Battle of Grunwald. The cost of a mercenary knight during this period was about 3 grosche of 16 skojec, so the war consumed huge sums. It is known from the pay book that after the battle, on July 20, 1,427 armed men came to Malbork asking to be paid for their participation in the war.

Istud est vexilium magistri generalis Henrici de Plawyen et sui ordinis cruciferorum, sub quo unico exercitus suus ad opidum Koronow die Veneris... pugnans fortissime conflictus est (...). Banderium magistri Livonie ordinis cruciferorum, quod Theodoricus Croe, ducebat... circa villam Sambky iusta fluvium Wyrzscha (...). Banderia Livonica... ab exercitu Polonico in campis Sambky captum in prelio (...).

The banner of the Great Master Henry von Plauen and his order, under which his army fought valiantly near the town of Koronowo (...). The banner of the Livonian Master, led by Marshal Theodoric von Croe in the battle near the village of Dąbki on the Wyrza River (...). Livonian banners captured by the Polish army in the fields of the village of Dąbki (...).

Those were captured banners in subsequent to Grunwald battles and conflicts, which later were also hung in the Krakow cathedral together with the trophies from Grunwald already there. The first of them (in „Banderia Prutenorum" it is listed as 47) was the gonfanon of Heinrich von Plauen captured in the battle of Koronowo on October 10, 1410. The next four are the banners of the Teutonic army from Livonia, captured in the battle of Dąbki on September 13, 1431 which went down in history as the victory of peasant infantry over seven Order commanders. Livonian Marshal Werner von Nesselrode led several hundred armed men, ravaging Krajna, Dobrzyn and Kujawy. They were opposed by the knights of Wielkopolska: Jan Jarogniewski, Bartosz Wezenbork and Dobrogost of Kolno, at the head of units composed of peasants. After the victorious fight, four Livonian banners along with the banner of the Livonian Marshal fell into Polish hands.

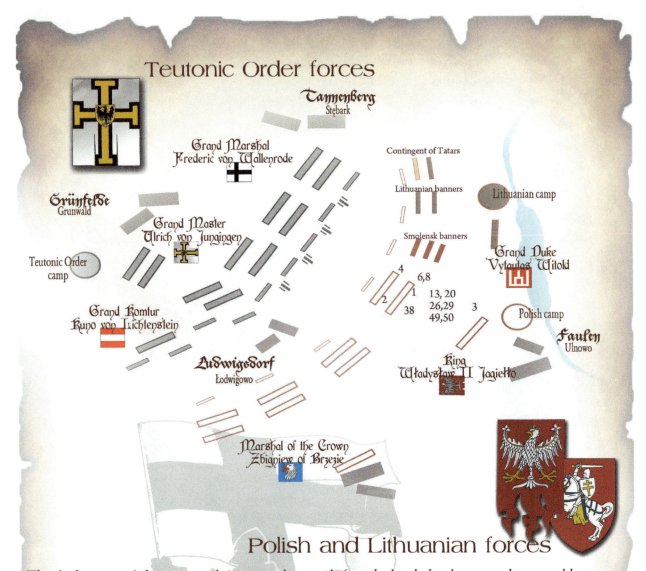

The deployment of the opposing banners and armies before the battle has been nearly impossible to ascertain and today it is clearly conjectural. Please note that the precise location of the battlefield still is not known for certain and a subject of numerous disputes and controversies.

However, in case of the Polish-Lithuanian army, is it possible to generally indicate the placement of banners within the deployed forces, with a degree of higher probability. The king's army was divided into three divisions: center and left and right wings. Crown Marshal Zbigniew of Brzezie commanded the left wing, which as we know consisted of the Wielkopolska Land banners,, the center of the army consisted of the Małopolska land banners, and the right wing was made up by the Lithuanian, Ruthenian and Tatar banners. The space between the army center and the right wing was held by the prestigious royal 'goncza-Renn' or 'dueling' banner and the St. George banner, the latter composed of Czechs and Moravian knights and mercenaries, groupped with additional mercenary Bohemian, Moravian and Silesian banners.

The battlefield array of the Teutonic Knights army at the joining of the battle can only remain in the realm of guesswork. They believe that the left wing of the Order's army was commanded by Grand Marshal Frederick von Wallenrode, and the right wing by Grand Commander Kuno von Lichtenstein.

Probably each army was arrayed into at least several battle-lines consisting of banners and had reserve banners in the rear or at ready, while additionally the Teutonic Knights also had fielded a few cannons deployed in a forward and fixed positions with their infantry opposite king's right wing. Both armies had wagon trains to the rear and behind their arrayed battle-ready units.

Banners of the Kingdom of Poland and the Grand Duchy of Lithuania

15th July 1410

July 15, 1410

In a great battle, numerous detachments of Polish chivalry, Lithuanian, Ruthenian and Tatar warriors and knights defeated the brother-monks of the Teutonic Order and their chivalrous Western European guests and mercenaries, as a sign of victory, collected numerous battle banners of the completely routed enemy from the battlefield!

The army of the union of the Kingdom of Poland and the Grand Duchy of Lithuania was divided into fifty-one Polish and forty Lithuanian-Ruthenian-Tatar banners. They also included banners of mercenary knights and men-at-arms, hired for money most often in Bohemia, Moravia and Silesia.

Most of the Polish knights and men-at-arms who set out with the king on the Prussian expedition in 1410 were the coat-of-arms nobility residing in the lands of the Kingdom and grouped in landed (20) clan banners or those issued by Crown civil and church officials and dignitaries obliged by duty and office. According to the military doctrine of the then Poland and still the greater part of Europe, the main forces of the army were the knights of the levy, who were somehow obliged to respond at the call of the ruler. As a rule, they were more or less „well-outfitted", i.e. suitably armored lancers with a few lighter armed squires and retainers. Such a chivalric unit was, just like in the case of the Teutonic Knights, called a lance. It should be noted that the armament of the Polish Army at that time did not differ from the armament of the Teutonic army, or Western European knighthood in general. Certainly, this was not any uniform armament, but it depended on the wealth and means of the knight, because the cost of the equipping of the lance and retinue was huge.

The organization of the Lithuanian army probably did not differ much from that of the Crown's banners. Duke Vitoldus, according to Długosz, the chronicler, divided his people into forty banners, which also included landed banners, 10 court banners and Tartars. It is estimated that there could be even 7-8 banners of the latter, which gave a number of 1,000-3,000 warriors, although the chronicler, probably due to the political correctness of those times, greatly underestimated the number of „Tatar pagans" aiding the Polish king and his vassals in the fight against the Christian Order.

On July 9, the allied forces crossed the border of the Teutonic State and unfurled their banners! The most important out of all of them was the great banner of Krakow Land displaying a white eagle with outstretched wings, and a golden crown on its head. It was treated as the emblem of the entire Kingdom.

The appearance of the remaining allied banners is known only from the descriptions provided by Jan Długosz in his „Annales." The banners themselves nor their mages have not survived, unlike those of the opposing side known from „Banderia Prutenorum." However, since their iconography was based mainly on the coats of arms of the Polish chivalry or the emblems of the Crown lands and territories belonging to the Kingdom, then with a degree a high probability today they can be recreated. However, it should be remembered that the Polish heraldry has also undergone many changes over the centuries.

Coats of arms, banners facilitated the identification of individual warriors in the turmoil of battle, appeared in Western Europe as early as the 12th century, while in Polish Piast realm they began to function starting in the 13th century. It should be noted that similar or even the same emblems could have been found in many countries, and they certainly were not dissimilar in the opposing armies fighting at Grunwald. It is also worth adding that, while, the number of coats of arms in the Polish Kingdom was quite limited, often many families or clans used the same or slightly modified emblem, while a completely different tendency was observed among the Western European chivalry. There, they could have as many coats of arms as there were knights.

For the knowledge of the nobility's coats of arms from the 15th-century Polish lands, three works are probably the most important. Jan Długosz's „Annals" already mentioned here, as well as his „Insignia seu clenodia Regis et Regni Poloniae", called „Jewels" in short, in which the author described in great detail the emblems of individual families and clans of Polish lands, and the „Armorials of the Golden Fleece" compiled by herald of the English King, Jean Lefevre de Saint Remy, in 1435 and presenting illustrations of over fifty heraldic emblems or coats of arms of the Polish chivalry and nobility of that 15th century period.

Much more difficult to accept and visualize are the Duchy of Lithuania flags, most of them, according to the chronicler, depicted images called Pogoń - an armored knight with a sword on a charging horse in various color variants. It can also be assumed that in addition to these Pogoń variants, some units may have had their own banners.

Habebat autem in exercitu custodum suorum, banderiolum, in quo erat pro insigni aquila alba, cuius signifer erat Nicolaus Morawiecz de Kynoszowka de domo Powala, exercitus autem ipse custodum sexaginta lances militum continebat (...).

He had a small pennon in his guard units, with the image of a white eagle, and which was carried by Mikołaj Morawiec of Kunoszówka, coat of arms Powała. The aforementioned guard banner contained 60 knightly lances (...).

Before the battle, they moved to protect the king, for „he himself alone was valued at ten thousand knights." In case of failure, horses were set up so that he could escape danger. Directly to protect the king, a small but select unit of brave knights was created under a small pennon with the image of a white eagle. Apart from the written description, no actual images of this flag have survived, so the appearance is hypothetical. It is known that on that faithful day king Władysław II was attended by, among others, the king's nephew by his sister, the Mazovian prince Siemowit the Younger, the Lithuanian princes Fieduszko and Zygmunt Korybutovich (king's nephew by his brother Dymitr Korybut), the Vice-Chancellors of the Kingdom of Poland Mikołaj Trąba, royal secretary Zbigniew of Oleśnica of the Dębno coat of arms, Jan Mężyk of Dąbrowa, the Czech lord Jan Solawa of Towacz clan, Henryk of Rogów, Zbigniew Czajka of Nowy Dwór, Dębno coat of arms, who carried the royal lance, Czech Jan Sokół and many others. As the story of the great battle tells Dypold Köckritz von Dieber, a guest knight in the service of the Order and of the Grand Master's close circle, famously charged alone against this very unit during the fateful final advance of those 16 banner Teutonic reserve led by the Grand Master through the battlefield, and von Kockritz was unhorsed and finally cut down by the royal bodyguards.

Primum vexilium magnum Cracoviensis terre, cuius alba aquila coronata extensis alis in campo rubeo erat insigne, in quo omnes prestanciores barones et milites Poloniae et omnes veterani et exercitati ordines acceperant, robore et numero omnia alia signa excedens; cuius ductor fuit prefatus Zindram de Maszkowicze ferentarius Marcissius miles de Wroczimowicze stirpis Palukosze...

The first was the Great Banner of the Land of Krakow, of which emblem was a white eagle with a crown and spread wings in a red field, in which all the most important Polish lords and knights, all veterans and those trained in battle had received their ranks, it surpassed all other banners in strength and number. Its commander was the aforementioned Zyndram of Maszkowice, and the standard-bearer was the knight Marcisz from Wrocimowice from the Polkozice clan…

The largest and most important banner in the Polish army was the banner of the Krakow Land, on the day of the battle probably located on the edge of the right wing of the royal army at the junction of the banners of Lesser Poland with the Lithuanian-Tatar contingent. Not only Cracovians fought in its ranks, but also the most illustrious knights from all over the kingdom. Długosz listed the most distinguished knights: Zawisza Czarny of Garbów, of Sulima clan, Floriana of Korytnica, Jelita coat of arms, Domarat of Kobylany, Grzymalita clan, Skarbek of Góra, Habdank clan, Paweł Złodziej of Biskupice, Niesobia clan, Jan Warszowski Nałęcz, Stanisław of Charbinowice, from the Sulima clan, and Jaksa of Targowisko, Lis clan. The Kraków banner with its white crowned eagle in red field - a symbol of the whole kingdom — and the emblem situated perpendicularly to the shaft was a gonfanon, thus marking the most important unit within the royal army just like its counterpart — the black cross in white field - of the Teutonic Knights' army.

Secundum vexillum Goncza, cuius due cruces cerulee in campo celestino erat insigne; id Andreas Brochocicze miles de domo Ozoria ducebat.

The second banner was a Goncza, which emblem was two crosses on a blue field; was carried by Andrzej of Brochocice, a knight of the Ozoria coat of arms.

It is not known exactly what the purpose of the Goncza (dueling, jousting or Rennen) banner was. Previously they believed that messengers delivering orders could have served in it, but this view has long been refuted. This banner belonged to the group of the most important court banners, and although it was less numerous in number of lances than the Kraków one, yet equally illustrious knights mustered under its emblem. Probably the name came from the knightly duel or Rennen, i.e. the knightly duel before the start of the battle. Perhaps this banner served as an advance guard. The double cross in the emblem was a personal royal sign recognized as a emblem of the Jagiellonian dynasty. In the royal battle formations at Grunwald, this banner occupied a central place together with the Bohemian-Moravian banner of St. George and four to six other banners near the right wing of the Polish army, at the junction with the Lithuanian-Tatar forces and the remainder of the Lithuania-Ruthenian army of the leftwing. The entire Banner group of this sector was commanded by the Crown Marshal Zbigniew of Brzezie. Długosz mentioned several antesignani knights by their names: Jan Sumik of Nabroż, Bartosz and Jarosz of Płomykowo from the Pomian clan, Dobiesław Okwia of the Wieniawa clan, and Bochemian knight Zygmunt Pikna, who died in battle.

Tercium cubicularium, cuius vir armatus equo candido insidens gladium quoque manu vibrans in campo rubeo erat insigne; id Andreas Czolek de Zelechow de domo Taurorum, Joannes de Sprowa de domo Odrowasch ducebant.

The third court banner had in the emblem a man in armor astride a white horse and brandishing a sword in a red field; this was led by Andrzej Ciołek of Żelechów, coat of arms Ciołek, and Jan of Sprowy, coat of arms Odrowąż.

Cubicularium was a court banner in which royal courtiers and members of the royal court served. In its first row fought knights famous in Poland at that time, including Mszczuj of Skrzynno, Łabędź coat of arms, Aleksander Gorajski, Korczak coat of arms, and Mikołaj Powała of Taczów. This court banner provided a protective screen to the royal bodyguard detachment around the king that would be threatened by the Grand Master's reserve advancement in the last, decisive phase of the great battle.

Quartum sancti Georgii habens crucem albam in campo rubeo pro insigni sub quo omnes Bohemi et Moravi precio conducti (cuius ductores erant Sokol et Zbislawek ad Bohemi, ferentarius vero Joannes Zarnowski Bohemus (...)) consistebant.

Fourth Banner of St. George with a white cross on a red field, under which were all mercenary Czechs and Moravians, the commanders were the Czechs Sokół and Zbysławek, and the banner was carried by Jan Sarnowski.

While there were serious reservations about the colors of the banners of St. George on the side of the Teutonic Knights, there can be no doubts here, because otherwise Mikołaj Trąba, Deputy Chancellor of the Crown, would not have confused it with the banner of Dobiesław of Oleśnica with almost the same colors. The mercenary banner located on the right wing of the Polish army belonged to the group protecting Crown Marshal Zbigniew of Brzezie. During the great battle, Czech and Moravian mercenaries twice left the ranks during the actual combat. The first time before the battle was joined, and the second time after the collapse of the Lithuanian wing of the allied army. There was even a suspicion that the ensign Sarnowski had been bribed by the Teutonic Knights. The Deputy Chancellor Mikołaj Trąba encountered this mercenary banner hiding in a birch forest, harangued them and with shaming words forced them to return to the battlefield. According to the chronicle, the ashamed knights abandoned their cowardly standard-bearer, marshaled their ranks and resumed combat in the great battle.

Quintum terre Posnaniensis albam aquilam in campo rubeo non coronatum habens pro insigni. Septimum Calisiense caput bubali in scacorum tabula diademate regio ornatum, ex cuius naribus circulus rotundus pendebat, habens pro insigni.

The fifth of the Poznań land, with the emblem of a white eagle without a crown in a red field. The seventh from Kalisz with the head of an auroch as a coat of arms in a chequer field decorated with a royal crown, from which nostrils hung a ring.

Both banners came to the Grunwald fields from Wielkopolska and were most likely positioned on the outer left flank of the armies of the Kingdom of Poland. It is assumed that the Crown land banners could have numbered about 500 people each. A standard bearer of the Poznań land banner was a knight of the Jelita coat of arms (blazon - in the red field two golden lances forming an oblique cross, and the third golden lance positioned vertically upside down on top of the two at their junction). This is one of the oldest Polish coats of arms, according to the heraldic legend, given to the family of the seriously wounded Florian Szary for his bravery during the battle of Płowce 1331 by King Władysław Łokietek on the battlefield. The standard-bearer of Kalisz had the Pobóg coat of arms (a silver - argent - horseshoe with a same color small cross on its arch) painted on the horse's surcoat.

Sextum Sandomiriensis terre, in quo pro una medietate tres barre seu tractus glauci in campo rubeo, pro altera septum stelle in campo celestino habebatur insigne. Octavum terre Siradiensis, in quo pro una medietate medietas aquile albe in campo rubeo, pro altera mediatas leonis flamei in campo albo habebatur insigne.

The sixth banner of the Sandomierz Land had a coat of arms in which on one half there were three yellow beams, i.e. notches on a red field, and on the other seven stars on a blue field. The eighth of the Sieradz Land had a coat of arms, in one half of which there was a half of a white eagle on a red field, and in the other half a flaming lion on a white field.

Both land banners could have been arrayed on the right wing of the Crown army and with high probability they took part in the attack on the Teutonic banners returning from the pursuit of fleeing Lithuanian detachments. The standard-bearer of the Sandomierz Land was a knight of the Nowina coat of arms (in the blue field a silver cauldron handle with its ends upwards, between them a sword thrust down), and the Sieradz land standard bearer had the Szeliga coat of arms (in the red field a golden crescent, with the corners turned upwards, in the center a Latin cross of the same color).

Nonum terre Lublinensis cervum cornibus extentis in campo rubeo habens pro insigni. Decimum terre Lanciciensis, cuius insigne media pars nigre aquile, medio vero albi leonis in campo ceruleo capita habentes coronata.

The ninth banner of the Lublin Land had a deer with spreading antlers on a red field as its coat of arms. The tenth of the Łęczyca Land, which in its coat of arms had half a black eagle and half a white lion with a crown on a yellow field.

In "The Jewels" Długosz described the Lublin Land deer as standing upright with a crown on his neck. No image of the then emblem of the Lublin Land has survived. Other colors than in „Annales" are given in the description of the flag of the Łęczyca Land. There was a red lion on a white field and a white eagle on a red field. Nothing is known about the placement in the army's array of these banners at Grunwald. Generally speaking, the position of about ten banners from the 51 banner of the Crown of Poland's army present on the battlefield can be given with high probability. The standard-bearer of the Łęczyca Land had a horse caparison covered in the colors of the Zabawa clan (a double-field shield divided vertically, the right field blue, the left field checkered red and silver), and the heavy-armed lancer in the middle had the Gozdawa coat of arms (in a red field, silver double lily flowers with a golden ring in the middle).

Undecim terre Cuiaviensis, in quo pro una mediatate aquile nigre in campo ceruleo mediatas, pro altera medietas leonis albi in campo rubeo capita coronata gestantes erat insigne.

Duodecimum terre Leopoliensis, leonem ceruleum per mediam petram conscendentem in campo celestino habens pro insigni.

The eleventh banner of Kujawy Land had a coat of arms with half a black eagle on a yellow field in one half, and a white lion on a red field with crowns on the other half.

The twelfth banner for the Lwów Land, had as its coat of arms a yellow lion climbing a rock on a blue field.

Half lion, half eagle is a characteristic motif of the Kuyavian, Łęczyca and Sieradz lands. It appeared on the seals of the Piast dukes ruling in this district of Polish lands as early as the second half of the 13th century in various color variants and in a different arrangement of the elements of the emblem. Also, in his works Długosz gave quite divergent colors of this coat of arms. The emblem of the Lwów Land certainly came from the Ruthenian lands and could have been brought to the canon of Polish coats of arms around the 14th century.

The standard-bearer of the Kuyavian land wore the Pilawa coat of arms on his jack (a three-part silver cross in the blue field) established for the ancestor of the family, who in the times of Bolesław Krzywousty defeated the Prussian champion in a duel in the village of Pilawa. The spear-armed knight had one of the oldest Polish noble coats of arms, Ostoja (in the red field two crescents pointing up, between an increscent and a decrescent a cross in pale point downwards). Tre-

decimum terre Wielunensis lineam niveam transversalem in campo rubeo proporcionaliter locatam habens pro insigni, cui rex propter raritatem ordinum milites ex Silesia mercenaries pro supplemento adiumxerat.

The thirteenth banner from Wieluń Lands, having in its coat of arms a transverse line of snow-white suitably placed on a red field. Due to the thinness of its ranks, the king supplemented it with mercenary knights from Silesia.

The banner of the Wieluń Lands, next to Halicz, Sandomierz and Krakow, probably took part in the attack on the Order's banners after the collapse of the Lithuanian wing. In addition to the knights from the Wieluń Land, mercenaries from Silesia, Bohemia and Moravia also fought there. The most famous participant in the battle fighting under this banner was Jan Długosz from Niedzielsk, of the Wieniawa coat of arms (a black bison head in a golden field with a golden ring in its nostrils), who was in fact the chronicler's father. During the fight, he took prisoner, apart from many others, the Brandenburg Commander Markward von Salzbach, the Samogitian Bailiff Schonburg and Grand Master's companion Jurga Marschalk. Jan Długosz handed them over to Grand Duke Vitoldus, who in turn ordered them beheaded, supposedly for insulting his mother during the congress on the Niemen River. The heavy-armed knight in the foreground may have been the commander of the banner, Bieniasz of Biała, the royal steward of the Wieruszów coat of arms (in a silver field, a goat standing, half black from the head and front legs, the other half checkered with red and white fields).

Quartum decimum terre Premisiensis, quod aquilam ceruleam duo capita a se invicem proporcionaliter aversa in campo celestino habebat pro insigni.

Quintum decimum terre Dobrinensis faciem humanam serilem ad femur se protendentem capite diademate adornato cornibus quoque exasperato in campo ceruleo habens pro insigni.

The fourteenth banner of the Przemyśl Lands, which had a yellow eagle with two heads respectively turned away from each other on a blue field as its coat of arms.

The fifteenth of banner of the Dobrzyń Lands had in its coat of arms on a yellow field the head of an old man with a crown and also made wild looking with horns pointed downwards, which added to its severity.

No exact image of the eagle from the Przemyśl banner has survived. It is known only from the description. However, the emblem of Dobrzyń Land and often in other primary sources the colors appeared different. The head in the emblem supposedly represented king Casimir the Great, who in 1343 restored this land which had been occupied by the Teutonic Knights to the Kingdom of Poland. In the background the lance-armed knight from this banner was a knight of the Wczele coat of arms (a black/silver and gold chessboard, although there were different color variations).

Sextum decimum terre Chelmensis ursum album inter duas arbores consistentem in campo rubeo habens pro insigni.

Vicesimum terre Haliciensis monedulam nigram in capite coronatam in campo albo habens pro insigni.

The sixteenth banner of the Chelm Land had a white bear standing between two trees on a red field as its coat of arms.

The twentieth banner of the Halych Land had a black jackdaw with a crown on its head on a white field as its coat of arms.

Halicz-Włodzimierz Ruthenia was a Polish Crown district in the borderlands between the Polish Crown, Hungarian Crown and Duchy of Lithuania. It was established after the disintegration of Kievan Rus with important centers at Halicz, Włodzimierz Wołyński, Brześć, Chełm, Lwow and Przemyśl. In the Middle Ages, these lands and more further south were disputed areas between the Kingdom of Poland, Lithuania and the Kingdom of Hungary. This conflict finally ended after duke Jagiełło married Queen Jadwiga of Poland, became Wladyslaw II Jagiellon of Poland and independently took the Polish throne after her death. As the King of Poland he assumed the title of Prince of Rus, which emphasized the separate legal status of these territories inherited by the Kingdom of Poland from the last Halicz duke Jerzy Boleslav II of Mazovia and Halicz. This land which was also already inhabited by a large number of Polish knights, raised as many as seven banners at Grunwald: Lwów, Halicz, Chełm, Przemyśl, and three banners from Podolia. The only knight of these banners who was actually named by his name was Iwanko Suszyk of Romanów, a Ruthenian nobleman rewarded for bravery by the king on the battlefield. He received two villages in the Halicz Land, awarded for shedding his blood and for bravery during the great battle. The Chełm Land banner's ensign had the Waldorff (Nabram) coat of arms.(Nabram) coat of arms.

17 18 19

Decimum septimum, decimum octavum et decimum nonum terre Podolie (tria enim signa abundante multitudine habebat) quorum quodlibet faciem solarem in campo rubeo habebat pro insigni.

The seventeenth, eighteenth and nineteenth banners of Podolia land; because of the great mass of knights, this land had three banners. Each of them had a sun disc on a red field in its coat of arms.

Geographically and historically, Podolia was a land located on the territory of today's Ukraine and Moldova. Already in the early Middle Ages, the entire area of Podolia came under the influence of the principality of Halych and Vladimir, and then in the course of the later 14th century became part of the Grand Duchy of Lithuania. Until 1402, this land was in the possession of king Wladyslaw II's brother, Prince Svidrigiello, who lost it when he entered into an alliance with the Teutonic Knights to fight for power against duke Vitoldus. In the years 1402–1411, on the basis of the Union of Vilnius and Radom, Podolia came again under the Polish Crown rule. On the banners, Długosz described the radiant sun, which was then as well as later the true emblem of this land. In „Annales" the sun appeared on a red field, but already in his work on heraldry „Insignia seu clenodia Regni Poloniae" and in a later woodcut from the times of king Kazimierz IV Jagiellon the background of the emblem was white. The knight in the background has the Kierdeja coat of arms on the shield, and the antesignan knight was a knight of the Świerczek coat of arms (in the blue field a golden capital letter N with a bend in the crossbeam).

Vicesimum primum et vicesimum secundum ducis Semaviti Masovie aquilam albam diademate in campo rubeo habencia pro insigni.

The twenty-first and twenty-second banners were those of the Mazovian prince Siemowit had a white eagle without a crown on a red field as the emblem.

The Masovian duke Siemowit IV, as a member of the Piast dynasty, was in the second half of the 14th century a serious contender for the hand of Queen Jadwiga of Anjou and the throne of the Kingdom of Poland that he had been striving for being supported by the Archbishop of Poland Bodzanta of Gniezno. In his efforts, during the interregnum after the death of King Ludwik he even went so far as to attempt to sneak in the Wawel Castle at Krakow and to abduct and marry the future queen, and when in this attempt they had failed, he declared himself a king and went to war against the Anjou supporters, but his plans was eventually derailed by the Malopolska-Hungarian army commanded by king Sigismund of Luxembourg of Hungary and loss of support in Wielkopolska and in Masovia of his elder brother prince Janusz I Starszy of Warsaw. The change in cirmcumstance, the crowing of queen Jadwiga az the ruler of Poland, forced new realities on this Piast duke, and he signed a treaty with the queen. After the Polish-Lithuanian personal union and marriage of the queen with Władysław II Jagiełło, the Masovian Piast prince renounced his rights to the Polish crown and concluded a trreaty with queen Jadwiga on 12th of December 1385, where in return for his support for royal couple and new king Władysław II, Siemowit received a land grant in the Bełsk Land in Halicz Ruthenia and the hand of the king's sister Aleksandra, and a huge sum of money. Despite paying the homage to the royal Polish rulers, for a long time he successfully navigated between Kingdom of Poland, Lithuania and the Order. Two Masovian banners from his dominion fought on the fields of Grunwald, but the duke himself did not take part in this campaign. He entrusted the command over them to his eldest son, Siemowit V. The noble knight from the Mazovian banner had the Pierzchała coat of arms on the shield, otherwise known as Roch or Kolumna.

Vicesimum tercium ducis Masovie Janussii, quod in quadrum divisum pro duabus medietatibus albam aquilam, pro reliquis duabus per trans versum se aspicientibus nocticoracem scacatum albi et rubei coloris habebat insigne.

The twenty-third banner was of Janusz, Duke of Mazovia, with his coat of arms, the field of which was divided into four parts, on two halves of a white eagle, and on the other two halves, cut in half and adjacent to each other, of a red eagle-owl.

Janusz I the Elder was the duke of Warsaw and Czersk and is considered one of the most outstanding Mazovian rulers. The duke encouraged close cooperation with the Kingdom of Poland, which was reflected in feudal homages paid to successive Polish monarchs. He opposed the policy of his brother Siemowit IV and was in almost constant conflict with the Teutonic Order. He was even kidnapped twice by brother-knights and freed only after the intervention of the Polish king. During the military campaign of 1410, the concentration of united Polish-Lithuanian armies occurred in his duchy near Czerwińsk. According to the chronicler, the description of the Mazovian flag of Prince Janusz may be inconsistent with its actual appearance. The coat of arms of the Czerwinsk Land was a dragon or a basilisk, while Długosz depicts an eagle-owl. The knight in the background had the Rola coat of arms on the shield, the second one had the Grzymała coat of arms, and the ensign carrying the prince's coat of arms came from the Rogala clan.

Vicesimum quartum Nicolai Kurowski archiepiscopi Gnesnensis fluvium cruce signatum in campo rubeo habens pro insigni.

Quadragesimum quintum Nicolai Kmithe de Wisnicze flumen rubeum cruce ornatum habens pro insigni.

The twenty-fourth banner of the Archbishop Mikołaj Kurowski of Gniezno had a river with a cross on a red field as its emblem.

Forty-fifth banner of Mikołaj Kmita of Wiśnicz had a white river with a cross on a red field in its coat of arms.

At the time of Grunwald, Mikołaj Kurowski was the Archbishop of Gniezno and Poland and from 1394 he was the Chancellor of the Kingdom of Poland. He took part in numerous legations to Malbork, the capital of the Order's state. One of his most important achievements was accomplished during his diplomatic legation after the outbreak of the uprising in Samogitia in 1409, when the Grand Master asked whether the Polish King would not help the Samogitian and Lithuanian insurgents, Archbishop replied that Poland would not leave Lithuania and in the event of war „our king would visit Prussia with force." Thanks to the Archbishop's gamble, it was the Teutonic Knights who declared war on Poland, which at that time was extremely important both for the internal royal policy and the perceived public relations image abroad. During the expedition to the Teutonic lands, the Archbishop stayed in Kraków, acting as the king's deputy for the duration of the war, but did send his banner to join the war. A similar emblem, Szreniawa, was on the coat of arms of Mikołaj Kmita of Wiśnicz, the voivode of Kraków, who took part in the battle commanding his own banner. The standard-bearer in the background had the Korczak coat of arms on his shield.

25 26

Vicesimum quintum Alberti Jastrzambiicz episcopi Posnaniensis babatum crucem habens i medio in campo celestino, cuius Jarandus de Brudzewo miles erat ductor, habens pro insigni.

Vicesimum sextum Cristini de Ostrow castelani Cracoviensis ursum virginem coronatam gestantem in campo rubeo habens pro insigni.

The twenty-fifth banner of Poznań's bishop, Wojciech Jastrzębiec, had a horseshoe with a cross in the middle on a blue field in its coat of arms.

The twenty-sixth banner of the Castellan of Kraków, Krystyn of Ostrów, had as its emblem a bear on a red field carrying a girl with a wreath on its head.

Wojciech Jastrzębiec was the Bishop of Poznań during the Great War. In 1401, he was a signatory of the Union of Vilnius and Radom, in which king Władysław II granted deputy powers in Duchy of Lithuania to Prince Vytautas, although the supreme power remained in the hands of the Polish king. In the years 1404 and 1408 he was a mediator in disputes with the Teutonic Knights. He took part in signing of the peace at Raciążek in 1404, that treaty 'bought' the Dobrzyń lands and town of Złotoryja from the Teutonic Knights and confirmed the Order's rights to Samogitia. Bishop Jastrzębiec did not take part in the great battle. According to the chronicle, he withdrew from the expedition, seeing the destruction of villages, towns and churches on the route of the Polish army. His deputy commander Jarand from Brudzew, Pomian coat of arms, commanded his bishopric banner. From 1406, Krystyn of Ostrów served as the voivode of Sandomierz, and in 1410 he became the Castellan of Kraków, the most important castellan office in the realm. Krakow Castellan raised his own banner flying his own emblem, called Rawa, Rawicz or Bear, for the great war against the Order. The coat of arms – a girl riding a bear – always appeared in a yellow field, but in „Annales" Długosz spoke of a red field.

27 37 39

Vicesimum septimum Joannis Tharnowski palatini Cracoviensis lunam cornutam stellam complectantem in campo celestino habens pro insigni.

Tricesimum septimum Vincencii de Granow castellani Srzemensis et Maiores Polonie capitanei, cuius luna arcuata stellam continens in medio in campo celestino erat insigne.

Tricessimum nonum Spytkonis de Jaroslaw, cuius luna arcuata stellam continens in medio in campo lazurino erat insigne.

The twenty-seventh banner of the voivode of Krakow, Jan Tarnowski, which had a horned moon embracing a star in the center on a blue field as its coat of arms.

The thirty-seventh of Wincenty of Granów, the castellan of Śrem and the starost of Wielkopolska, which coat of arms was a horned moon with a star in the middle on a blue field.

Thirty-ninth of Spytek of Jarosław, which coat of arms was a horned moon with a star in the center on an azure field.

All three flags feature the Leliwa coat of arms, which dated back to the 12th century. The first of the Leliwa banners was raised by the voivode of Krakow, Jan of Tarnów, which was the most important voivodeship in the realm. During the Great War, he was a member of the eight-member royal council advising the king.

The second flag of bearing this coat of arms belonged to Wincenty of Granów, the starost general of Greater Poland in the years 1409-1410. He was considered an expert on Teutonic affairs and was poisoned by the Teutonic Knights in 1410, some time before December 1410. His widow, Elżbieta of Pilcza, became king Władysław II Jagiełło's third wife on May 2, 1417. The third banner of the Leliwa clan was commanded by the Ruthenian starost and the voivode of Sandomierz, Spytek of Jarosław and Tarnów, Jan's brother. He was one of the most preminent and wealthiest dignitaries of the kingdom. After the Prussian war, his troops had guarded the southern border, and after the attack made on the southern Polish lands by the Hungarian army commanded by Ścibor of Ściborzyce, a Polish nobleman in the service of Sigismund of Luxembourg and ally with the Order, these Polish banners defeated the intruder in battle and aborted his invasion of the southern Poland.

Vicesimum octavum Sandivogii de ostrorog palatini Posnaniensis fasciam arcuatam et circumligatam et in extremitates protensam, in campo rubeo habens pro insigni.

Quadragesimum primum Dobrogostii de Schamotuli fasciam arcuatam et in medio constrictam in campo rubeo habens pro insigni.

The twenty-eighth banner of the voivode of Poznań, Sędziwoj of Ostrorog, had as its emblem a rolled kerchief bound in a circle with the ends spread on a red field.

Forty-first banner of Dobrogost of Szamotuły, had as its emblem a wavy kerchief tied in the middle on a red field.

Both banners belonged to the group of family banners, and their symbol was the Nałęcz coat of arms coming mainly from Wielkopolska, that belonged to the oldest coats of arms of the Polish nobility. From 1406, Sędziwój of Ostrorog held the office of the voivode of Poznań and was one of the king's most trusted advisers on the Lithuanian and Teutonic matters. In August 1399, Sędziwój and Dobrogost Świdwa of Szamotuły took part in the expedition of Prince Vitoldus against the Golden Horde Tatars. In the battle of Worskla River, the duke's forces were routed, and many good Polish knights killed. In 1410 Dobrogost, the castellan of Poznań, raised this banner for the Prussian war and forth months after the battle of Grunwald, on October 10, 1410, at Koronowo the banners of both Nałęcz lordds blockaded the path of the incoming Teutonic reinforcements led by Micheal Küchmeister von Sternberg, the Bailiff of the New March. The resulting Polish knights' victory of the Western knights in this cavalry battle contributed mightily to the signing of the Toruń peace treaty of 1411.

Vicesimum nonum Nicolai de Michalow palatini Sandomiriensis rosam albam in campo rubeo habens pro insigni.

Tricesimum Jacobi de Koniecpole palatini Siradiensis babatum album, infra porte pociori demissa, et cruce signatum in campo rubeo habens pro insigni.

The twenty-ninth banner of the voivode of Sandomierz, Mikołaj of Michałów, with a white rose on a red field as its coat of arms.

The thirtieth banner of voivode of Sieradz, Jakub of Koniecpol, had a white horseshoe hanging down, marked with a cross on a red field as its emblem.

Mikołaj of Michałów and Kurozwęki held the office of the starost of Sandomierz during the Prussian expedition. Earlier, together with Bishop Mikołaj Kurowski, he participated in the legation to Malbork, demanding the return of ships with grain sent to starving Lithuania and seized by the Order on the claim of carrying contraband arms to the Samogitians. Later, during the 1410 expedition, he was summoned by the king to join in the royal council, in which the most important dignitaries were councilors to the king. He also fielded his own banner but was with the king's retinue and bodyguards during the great battle. The white rose depicted on the flag was a clan crest called Poraj or Róża. Jakub of Koniecpol and Januszew held the office of the Voivode of Sieradz and the starost of Kujawy, he also served as the chamberlain of the court of Queen Sophia, king's second wife after the death of queen Jadwiga. During the great war, he was a member of the king's aforementioned council and also fielded his own banner, which he commanded in the great battle. The coat of arms on the banner is a clan symbol called Pobóg.

Tricesimum primum Joannis alias Iwan de Obychow castellani Srzemiensis caput Zubronis, a cuius naribus circulus rotundus dependens in campo croceo habens pro insigni.

Tricesimum secundum Joannis Ligreza de Bobrek palatini Lanciciensis, cuius caput asininum in campo rubeo erat insigne.

The thirty-first banner of Jan or Ivan of Obichów, the Castellan of Śrem, had a wisent's head with a round ring hanging from its nostrils in a yellow field as its coat of arms,.

Thirty-second of the voivode of Łęczyca, Jan Ligęza from Bobrek, whose emblem was a donkey's head on a red field.

Lord Jan (Iwo) from Obichow held the office of castellan of Śrem from 1408 and was one of the king's close advisers. At Grunwald, he commanded his own banner, the sign of which was the Moravian coat of arms of Iwo of Obichow called Wieniawa with the image of a wisent's head. This emblem was also the coat of arms of Jan Długosz.

Lord Jan Ligęza of Bobrek was the Voivode of Łęczyca in the years 1374-1418. At Grunwald, he raised and commanded his own banner, the emblem of which was the coat of arms of the Ligęza clan, called Półkozic. Lance-armed knight in the background had one of the medieval versions of the Ostoja coat of arms (in the red field two crescents pointing up, between an increscent and a decrescent a cross in pale point downwards) on his shield.

33 36

Tricesimum tercium Andree de Thanczin castellani Woiniciensis, cuius in campo rubeo una bipennis erat insigne.

Tricesimum sextum Clementis de Moszkorzow castellani Wisliciensis, cuius due cum dimidia cruces cerulee in campo flaveo erat insigne.

Thirty-third banner of Andrzej of Tęczyn, the castellan of Wojnicz, which coat of arms was an ax on a red field.

The thirty-sixth of Klemens of Moskorzów, the castellan of Wiślica,, which emblem was two and a half yellow crosses on a blue field.

Lord Andrzej of Tęczyn, from 1408 a deputy pantler of Krakow, belonged to one of the most powerful families in Malopolska. At Grunwald, he led his own banner under the Topór clan emblem, also known as Starża. According to Długosz, he was one of the knights who persuaded the king to break the siege of Malbork in September 1410, spreading a rumor that at the same time Hungarian troops invaded the southern borders of Poland. Royal Vice-Chancellor and the Castellan of Wiślica, lord Klemens of Moskarzew was one of the most important dignitaries at the royal court and in the kingdom. For the Prussian War, he raised his own banner with the Pilawa coat of arms.

Tricesimum quartum Sbignei de Brzezie Regni Polonie marsalci, cuius caput leoninum evomens flammam in campo celestino erat insigne.

The thirty-fourth banner of the Marshal of the Kingdom of Poland, Zbigniew of Brzezie, which emblem was a fire-breathing lion's head on a blue field.

Lord Zbigniew of Brzezie was one of the most important dignitaries at the royal court. From 1399 to his death in 1425, he was the Grand Marshal of the Crown, the highest-ranking commander of the Crown army. During the Prussian expedition, he belonged to the council supporting the king and was formally its deputy. At his command and order, army marching columns were formed, and the army moved in an organized fashion. At the head of the marching army was the marshal with the royal banner. Commanding several units, Zbigniew reconnoitered the enemy lines at dawn on July 15, when it was reported about the approaching Teutonic army and was probably supposed to hold back the Teutonic forces in case they would have advanced to attack until the Polish troops were arrayed in battle order. At Grunwald, Zbigniew of Brzezie also headed his own banner with the Zadora clan emblem, otherwise known as Płomień (Flame).

Tricesimum quintum Petri Schafraniecz de Pieskowa Skała succamerarii Cracoviensis, cuius albus equuus nigro tegmine in medio precintus in campo rubeo eratinsigne.

The thirty-fifth banner of t Piotr Szafraniec of Pieskowa Skała, the Kraków Chamberlain, which coat of arms was a white horse girted in the middle with a black blanket on a red field.

Lord Piotr Szafraniec, the Krakow chamberlain, was one of the most important people at the royal court, as evidenced by the fact that he was appointed to the „council of eight" to advise the ruler during the campaign of 1410. Earlier, he participated in negotiations with the Order, as a result of which, among others, the peace in Raciąż was signed in 1404, allowing Poland to buy back the Dobrzyń Land occupied by the Teutonic Knights and the castle in Złotoria together with its district for the amount of 2,400 kopecks of Czech groschen. At the same time under this treaty, duke Vitoldus confirmed the release Lithuanian dominion over Samogitia to the Teutonic Order. The banner of Piotr Szafraniec appeared in a great battle under the clan emblem known as Starykoń or simply Szafraniec.

Tricesimum octavum Sobeslai de Oeschnicza cruum albam, sub quarto crucis angula triplicem habens in modum duplicis W tracturam in campo rubeo pro insigni habens.

The thirty-eighth banner of Dobiesław of Oleśnica had a white cross in the coat of arms and in the fourth corner of the cross a double notch in the shape of the letter "W" on a red field.

Dobiesław of Oleśnica, Dębno coat of arms, was one of Władysław Jagiełło's trusted men. Already in the years 1393-1394 he was a valet at the court, served as a master of kitchens, imported sumptuous weapons, equipment and cloth for the king, and participated in royal legations and delegations. After signing the peace in Raciąż, at the tournament organized by the Great Master Konrad von Jungingen in Toruń, he became famous as its winner of the jousting, unhorsing all his opponents one by one, and his opponents were the most prominent guest-knights of the Order from all over of the Western Europe. For the Prussian War, Dobiesław raised his own banner under his own emblem. According to Długosz, when the Teutonic reserve appeared and the Polish knights were uncertain who they were faced with, he rode off alone to meet the advancing banners, and even was reported that he fought a lance duel with their commander, who might have been the Grand Master himself. Having suffered wounded horse during this joust, he withdrew back to the Polish line, but by his action he dispelled any doubts about nature of the approaching combatants.

Quadragesimum Martini de Sławsko superiorem partem leonis et quatuor lapides in parte inferiori habens pro insigni.

Banner forty of Marcin from Sławsko had the upper part of the lion's silhouette and four stones in the lower one in the coat of arms.

As the fortieth banner, Długosz mentions the clan banner of the Zaremba, one of the oldest in Wielkopolska. The coat of arms of Zaremba (Zaręba) supposedly dated back to the times of the Piast dynasty, but its oldest image that can be found on the seal of the bishop of Poznań belonged the beginning of the 14th century.

The description and image of this coat of arms can be found both in Długosz's "Jewels" and in the "Armorial of the Golden Fleece" published by the herald of the English king in 1435. This emblem occurs in several different varieties, both in terms of colors and arrangement of stones. From 1409, Marcin of Sławsko held the office of the Podstoli (deputy pantier) of Poznań and in the great battle commanded the clan banner of the Zaremba.

Quadragesimum secundum Cristini de Cozegłowy castelani Sandecensies sagittam geminatam cruce ornatam in campo rubeo habens pro insigni.

Quadragesimum septimum militis Zaklicze Korzegwiczski tracturam albam in modum duplicis V cruce signatam habens in campo rubeo pro insigni.

The forty-second banner of Krystyn of Koziggłowy, the castellan of Nowy Sącz, had an arrow decorated with a double cross on a red field in its coat of arms.

The forty-seventh of lord knight Zaklika Korzekwicki, had in its coat of arms a white emblem in the shape of a double V with a cross on a red field.

Krystyn of Koziggłowy the Younger was at the time of Grunwald the Castellan of Nowy Sącz and held the office of judge of Nowy Sącz. He was a dignitary and a politician, but he fielded his own banner for the Prussian Campaign, and it is very likely that he marched at its head. The coat of arms depicted on the banner was called Lis (also Mzuera, Buzra, Vulpes).

Zaklika of Korzkiew, the Castellan of Wiślica, came from a poor family in Malopolska, but at Grunwald he commanded his own banner. The chronicler did not record the actions of this knight during the battle, but his name appears in October 1410, when, on the orders of the king, he set out to meet the Teutonic reinforcements led by the Bailiff of the New March and contributed to the victory in the Battle of Koronowo.

Quadragesimum tercium Joannis Maszik de Dambrowa duos pisces, qui trutte apellantur, unum in campo albo, alterum in campo rubeo habens pro insigni.

The forty-third banner of Jan Mężyk from Dąbrowa which had two fish called trout as its emblem, one on a white field, the other on a red field.

Jan Mężyk of Dąbrowa was a trusted knight of King Władysław II. From 1404, he had held the offices of Cupbearer, a cubiularius or Butler, who was responsible for the royal bedrooms, also a Royal Secretary, and often he was sent as an envoy to neighboring countries on behalf of his monarch. At Grunwald, he raised own at his own expense his own banner, but he did not fight under it, as he was included in the personal retinue and bodyguard of the king. In „Annales" by Długosz, he appeared as the one who translated the message of the two Teutonic heralds who brought two naked swords from the Great Master to the Polish king. The emblem Jan Mężyk placed on his banner was the Wadwicz clan coat of arms. The lance-armed knight in the foreground was a knight from the Krakow Land, coat of arms Topór (Starża).

Quadragesimum quartum Nicolai Regni Polonie vicecancelarii tres tubas in campo albo habens pro insigni.

The forty-fourth banner of Mikołaj, the Deputy Chancellor of the Kingdom of Poland, had three trumpets on a white field as its coat of arms.

Mikołaj Trąba from Wiślicz, the Archbishop of Halicz, was one of the most trusted royal advisers. As Deputy Chancellor of the Crown and personal confessor of king Władysław II Jagiełło, he was constantly at his side. During the great battle, Długosz counted him among the monarch´s bodyguard and the „council of eight". After setting up the banners in battle order, Mikolaj Traba, together with other clergymen and scribes, was to go to the camps. On the way, he encountered a mercenary banner of Bohemians and Moravians hiding in the nearby forest and avoiding combat. As a result of the archbishop´s scolding but rousing speech, the knights abandoned their standard-bearer Jan Sarnowski and shamed by their unchivalrous conduct joined the fighting troops. During the siege of Malbork, he advocated staying under the walls of the fortress until it was reduced and conquered. In the years 1411-1422 he was the Archbishop of Gniezno and from 1418 he received the title of Primas Regni from Pope Martin V, the Primate of Poland. Probably on his initiative, „Cronica conflictus Wladislai Regis Poloniae cum Cruciferis anne Christi 1410", the first account and chronicle of the great war with the Order, was written down.

Quadragesimum scotum fratrum et militum Griffonum album griffonum in campo rubeo habens pro insigni; cuius ductor erat Sigismundus de Bobowa miles subiudex Cracoviensis.

The forty-sixth banner of the Gryf knights had a white griffon on a red field in their coat of arms. Its commander was a knight from Krakow, Zygmunt of Bobowa.

The forty-sixth banner in „Annales" is the ancestral banner of the Gryf clan inhabiting then the lands of Kraków and Sandomierz. Długosz named Zygmunt of Bobowa as its commander, but there are speculations that this was another mistake made by the chronicler. During the great battle, Sigismund was a rather unknown and a very young knight. It has been hypothesized that the banner could have been led by more experienced Gryf clan members, e.g. Krystyn Myszka of Nieprześna, who received a reward of 100 groschen from the king for his participation in the great war.

Quadragesimum octavum fratrum et militum Kozlerogi tres hastas transversaliter in campo rubeo deferencium; cuius ductor erat Florianus de Korythnicza castelanus Wisliciensis et in Przedpacz capitaneus.

Forty-eighth banner of the Koźle Rogi brothers, knights of that clan bearing in their coat of arms three spears folded crosswise on a red field. The commander was the castellan of Wiślica and the Staroste of Przedecz, Florian of Korytnica.

The forty-eighth banner was the clan banner of the Jelita bearing the Jelita coat of arms or otherwise known as Koźle Rogi (Goat Horns), represented by three lances. Długosz said that their commander was Florian of Korytnica, who served as the Cupbearer of Sandomierz, and later in the years 1407-1411 the Starost General of Ruthenia, but elsewhere in the book he places him as an antesignani knight of the Krakow Land banner. On the way back from Malbork, together with Piotr Chełmski of the Ostoja coat of arms, without waiting for an order to attack, they captured the castle in Radzyń Chełmiński, defended by the Teutonic Knights. During the so-called "Famine War" of 1414, Florian of Korytnica was still mentioned among the best knights of the Kingdom of Poland.

Quadragesimum nonum Joannis Jenczykowicz baronis de Moravia, quod albam sagittam distensam et in finibus recurvatam in campo rubeo, que aput Polonos Odrowansz nominatur, habebat pro insigni.

The forty-ninth banner of Jan of Jenczykowic, a lord from Moravia, had in its coat of arms a white arrow streched out and recurved at the ends on a red field, which the Poles call Odrowąż.

The forty-ninth banner was rather composed of mercenaries from Moravia, commanded by an unknown knight named Helm. The entire banner raised and sent to the king at his own expense by Jan of Jicin „as a favor" rendered to his family by king Władysław II Jagiełło. In the battle array these Moravian mercenaries could have been deployed on the extreme right wing of the Polish army next to the banner of St. George, at the junction with the Lithuanian-Ruthenian-Tatar banners. In Polish heraldry this emblem on the banner was called Odrowąż, while in Moravia it was called Benesz. Polish, Czech and Moravian coats of arms were often very similar at that time.

Quinquegesimum Gniewoschii de Dalyewicze subdapiferi Cracoviensis, quod sagittam albam in medio ad partem levam et dextram protensam cruce super protensione transversali consignatam in campo rubeo habebat pro insigni, sub quo tantummodo mercenarii milites non ex Polonis sed ex Bohemis, Moravis et Slesitis per profatum Gniewosium subdapiferum conducti militabant (...).

The fiftieth banner of Gniewosz of Dalewice, the Lord Cham of Krakow, who had in the coat of arms an arrowhead pronged on left and right with a cross in the middle above the transverse fork on a red field; only mercenary knights served in it, not from Poland, but recruited by the same Gniewosz among the Czechs, Moravians and Silesians (...).

Lord Gniewosz of Dalewice, coat of arms of Strzegom, before the start of the military operations in 1410, became the Lord High Stewart of Kraków, and even earlier he was the Marshal of the court of Queen Jadwiga. He was involved in some court intrigues, one being well chronicled in the sources. Namely, Gniewosz started an intrigue and spread gossip that, despite the marriage to king Wladyslaw II, queen Jadwiga was having an affair with William. Tried for his words by a Crown tribunal in Wiślica, Gniewosz was sentenced to barking-off as if a dog of his lies. The penalty, common in medieval Poland, forced Gniewosz to publicly prone himself under the table and announce that what he told about the queen was a dogly lie and to bark several times, and he did comply with the order As he belonged to the rich nobility during the Prussian war, he recruited his men-at-arms in Silesia, in Bohemia and Moravia, and at his own expense he raised a whole banner. Like the previous one, it could stand in the reserve of the Polish army behind the banner of St. George. On the banner tehere was the coat of arms of the commander called Kościesza or Strzegom, showing a pronged arrowhead with a cross in the middle.

Quinquagesimum primum Sigismundi Koributh Lithuanie ducis, quod equum armatum hominem gestans in campo rubeo habebat pro insigni.

The fifty-first flag of the Lithuanian prince Zygmunt Korybut had the coat of arms of a man in armor astride on a horse on a red field.

Prince Zygmunt Korybutowicz, son of Dymitr Korybut, Duke of Nowogród and Siewierz, who was king´s brother, nephew of King Władysław II Jagiełło, was probably just over 20 years old during the battle of Grunwald. His banner was placed by the chronicler among the mercenary Polish troops, as it was probably raised from some Polish mercenary knights. It is even possible that he did not command this banner, as he was mentioned in the „Annales" as a member of a detachment of the royal bodyguard. The emblem on the flag clearly represented the Pogoń, the coat of arms of the Grand Duchy of Lithuania already in the Middle Ages.

Erant pretera in exercitu Lithuanico Alexandri Withavdi ducis Magni Lithuanie quadraginta vexilla, sub quibus milites Lithuani, Rytheni, Samagite et Tartari tantumodo consistebant (...).

There were forty banners of the Lithuanian Grand Duke Alexander Vitoldus in the Lithuanian army, under which only Lithuanian, Ruthenian, Samogitian and Tatar knights appeared (...).

The Grand Duke of Lithuania brought his army divided into 40 banners according to the chronicler. Among them were 17 flags of the lands of Trakai, Vilnius, Grodno, Kaunas, Lida, Medininkai, Polotsk, Vitebsk, Kiev, Pińsk, Drohich, Mielnik, Nowogródek, Wołkowysk, Brest, Krzemieniec, Starodubsk, as well as banners of Lithuanian dignitaries, such as prince Simeon Lingwen with a banners from Nowogród and Pskov, starost of Wilno Moniwid or duke Ivan Żedewid Koriatowicz. The emblem of these banners was the sign of the Pogoń, characteristic for Lithuania, in Lithuanian 'Vytis,' depicting a knight with a sword on a horse in various color variants, equally of figure, background and details. The figure of a horseman with a raised sword appeared already in the 13th century on the seals of Alexander Nevsky, and the first ruler of Lithuanian descent known in history, who used such a coat of arms was Gleb Narymunt, the firstborn son of the Grand Duke Gedimunas of Lithuania in the 14th century.

Decem tantumodo signum aliud habebant et a triginta aliis distinguebantur, in quibus in campo rubeo signa, quibus Withaydus equos, quorum multitudine abundabat, insignire consueverat, depicta erant, que quidem in hunc modum, quoniam rebus describi non possunt, pingebantur.

Ten of them had a different emblem and were different from the other thirty. There were images painted on them on a red field, with which Vitoldus used to mark horses, and he had lots of them. These emblems were painted in such a way that they could be described.

Duke Alexander Vitoldus Kiejstutowicz, who was baptized with the name of Alexander, was the cousin of the Polish King serving as the governor of Lithuania from 1392 - 1401, and from 1401 onwards as the Grand Duke of Lithuania. His princely rule was a continuous series of actions and deeds intended to make Lithuania a strong and independent state with himself at the helm. He fought at that time with Duchy of Moscovy, the Golden Horde and the Teutonic Knights, often making and changing alliances and sides. In 1401 he signed the Union of Vilnius and Radom, thanks to which in March 1401 he received in Radom from the Polish king and his lords the title of the Grand Duke of Lithuania for life but remained the subject to the Polish ruler. Since then, he assumed the title of „Supreme Duke of Lithuania" (Supremus Dux Lituaniae). During the great battle, out of forty banners, probably ten were directly moderately subordinated to Witold's authority. The images of these troops were the second historical emblem of Lithuania - the Pillars of Gediminus, which appeared on his princely seal as early as around 1397.

In eo conflictu Smolensium milites Rutheni ad tria propria consistentes signa pertinacius pugnando soli fuge expertes insignem laudem meruerant. nam etsi sub signo uno cesi forent durissime et signum usque humo perculcatum, in duobus tamen reliquis, quemadmodum viros et milites conveniebat, fortissime pugnando victores evaserant seque tandem polonicis agminibus coniunxerant solique in exercitu Alexandri Withawdi laudem dimicacionis tulerant fortis et heroice illo die. Ceteri omnes, relictis in dimicacione Polonis, curso effuso ad fugam hoste persequente ferebantur.

In this struggle, the Ruthenian knights from Smolensk, standing with three of their own banners and fighting bravely, had earned deservedly a great deal of glory as the only ones who did not take part in the escape. Though under one banner they were cut down in the cruelest manner, and the banner was trampled on the ground, in the other two, they fought bravely, as befitted men and knights, they emerged victorious and joined the Polish hosts, and were the only ones to receive praise from Alexander Vitoldus' army for fighting bravely and heroically on that day. All the rest, leaving the Poles in the engagement, were driven and carried away to chaotic flight by the pursuing enemy.

At Grunwald, Alexander Vitoldus' army had three Smolensk banners: Smolensk, Smolensk-Orsza and Smolensk-Mścisław. The chronicler did not give the precise description of their banners, but only places them among other Lithuanian units with the emblem of Pogoń. We know and are certain that in the battle array and formation before the engagement the Smolensk banners were deployed on the left flank of the prince's army, in point of contact with the Polish banners. We also are certain that they did not run away from the battlefield when the Lithuanian army collapsed and they had to fight almost a suicidal action in order to keep their unity and cohesiveness and to brake through the increasing pressure of the attacking Order's units, thus sustaining huge losses in dead and wounded, to finally join the Polish lines, which they did manage and continued the battle among the Polish banners.

Transitu et superato flumine Wisla pontis navalis beneficio Wladislaus Polonie rex stativa sua ad alteras ripas eiusdem fluminis Wisla ponit. In que die eodem dux magnus Lithuanie Alexander cum gentibus suis et Tartarorum imperatore trecentos tantummodo tartaros habente in suo comitatu advenit.

After crossing the Vistula River on a pontoon bridge, the Polish King Władysław sets up a camp on the other bank of the Vistula River. On the same day, the Grand Duke of Lithuania, Alexander, arrived with his troops and the Tatar Khan, who had only three hundred Tatars with him.

On the fields of Grunwald, within the army of Lithuanian Grand Duke Vitoldus, also appeared some Tatar banners, led by the prince Vitoldus' vassal Jalal ad-Din, son of deposed Golden Horde khan Tokhtamysh and a pretender to the throne of the Golden Horde, a Mongol state founded circa 1240 in the western part of Genghis Khan's empire, which had been destabilized by numerous civil wars throughout the 14th century and early 15th century. In the struggle for his father's throne khan Jalal ad-Din had been defeated in the steppe and took refuge with his lords, warriors and retainers and their families in the Grand Duchy of Lithuania, becoming duke's ally in exchange for a promise to aid him in regaining the khanate's throne. Długosz stated that there were „only three hundred" Tatars during the campaign, but today's historians assume that it could have been as many as 1,000 to 3,000 warriors and retainers. In enumerating of the Lithuanian banners, the chronicler lists 33 out of forty units, so the seven missing may have been the Tatar banners. The entry in „Annales" was probably nothing more than to mark their presence, because it was not proper for a Christian king to use pagans against the Order.

Calendarium

it is a long way
from Akka to Grunwald

it is a long way
from Akka to Grunwald

In 1190, during the siege of Acre, a group of burghers from Bremen and Lübeck founded a hospital to provide care for wounded German crusaders.

On March 5, 1198, during a council of the German crusaders with the barons of the Kingdom of Jerusalem, they decided that the German hospital should be militarized and turned into a knightly monastic order. The first named Teutonic master was a former Templar, Herman Walpot.

1210-1220 The Prussians, acting against the Christianization campaign by Catholic Church and the Polish Pomeranian and Masovian dukes' attempts of expansion, responded by organized raiding and depredations. War-bands and even small armies led by the Prussian warlords attacked Polish Christians of Pomerania, Masovia, Kuyavia and Chełmno Lands.

In 1211, at the invitation of the Hungarian King Andrew II, the Teutonic Knights settled in eastern Transylvania known as the Burzenland. They are to defend the borders against the invasions of nomadic Cuman tribes.

1018 – Cistercian monk Christian of Oliva and the bishop of Prussia received the Chełmno Land from duke Konrad of Masovia. Bishop Christian organized a military Order of Dobrzyn to aid and defend his missionary efforts in the pagan Prussian lands. Town of Grudziac becomes bishop's de facto capital.

On April 30, 1224, upon Hermann von Salza's insistence Pope Honorius III issued a bull by which the lands of the Burzenland were to be excluded from the Hungarian jurisdiction and became de jure Church property.

1225 upon his nobles insistence King Andrew II of Hungary, freshly arrived from the 5th Crusade, without any warning marched into the Teutonic Knights' domain and expelled them out of Burzenland. He also demanded that they reimburse the Crown for 1,000 grzywna of unduly levied taxes on his subjects. To investigate the case, the pope sent three trusted Cistercians, but the king did not wait for their verdict and completely removed the Teutonic Knights from the Burzenland.

1208-20 various Polish dukes, upon suggestions from their bishops and German relatives, invited the Teutonic Knights into various towns and rural areas of their respective realms to built strongholds, develop and protect the lands, starting with duke Henry the Bearded of Silesia who promoted monastic orders of Templars, Hospitallers and now the Teutonic Knights.

1228-30 Konrad of Mazovia invited the Teutonic Knights to his realm to defend his borderlands against the Prussians' raids and incursions and to aid in Christianization of the pagan Prussians. The same year 1228 in the privilege of Lowicz duke Konrad granted town of Dobrzyn and Dobrzyn Land to the Order of Dobrzyn Knights.

In 1230, the Teutonic Knights begun their own negotiations with Bishop Christian of Prussia and Chelmno Land. He was the papal representative in the whole Prussia and no crusader army, even monastic ones, could have attempted to enter the pagan lands without his consent. In exchange for the martial aid and protection in the Christianization of the Prussians and for the protection of Prussian converts against pagan attacks, the bishop transferred his estates in the Chełmno Land and Michałowski Land to the Order!

On January 18, 1230, the Teutonic Knights submitted a forged document, falsely claiming duke Konrad had issued this privilege to the Order, to Pope Gregory IX granting the Order authority over the Chełmno Land and its conquests in Prussia - the so-called Kruszwica Privilege. The Pope approved the agreement with a bull, with the proviso that the princely grant concerns pagan lands where the Christian faith has not yet been introduced.

1230-1231 year. The Teutonic Knights under the command of the Master of the Order Herman von Balk crossed the Vistula River and conquered the area of Chełmno. Then they rebuilt Chełmno and built Toruń.

1233 -1240. Three Baltic crusades ravaged Prussia. Crusaders from all over Europe take part in them, but it is mainly German princes and knights and merchants from Lübeck, Bremen and other cities of northern Germany.

1234 Margrave of Meissen, Henry, invited by Konrad Mazovia for a crusade against the Prussians, invaded instead city of Płock, the capital of the Duchy of Masovia, and burned the ducal cathedral. At the same time, the Teutonic Knights, without Konrad's consent and knowledge, incorporated by agreement the Dobrzyn Knights and their domain, i.e., the Dobrzyn Land. The exemplary cooperation of the Teutonic Knights with Konrad of Masovia thus ended, but duke being busy with this quest for the Polish throne down south did not purse any hostile actions against them

1234-1238. The Teutonic Knights successively conquer Pogezania - the land of bushes (they build Elbląg there), Natangia - the land of flowing waters, Warmia - the red land and the land of the Bartians. The defeated Prussians are recruited by the Teutonic Knights into the Teutonic army and forced to fight in the interests of the occupiers.

1234 The Golden Bull of Rieti – Papal bull by Gregory IX giving the Order domination over the Chemno Land east of the Vistula and any land conquered by the Order in Prussia for 'eternal and absolute ownership.'

1235. The Golden Bull of Rimini – a decree by Emperor Fredric II giving and granting the privilege of conquest and territorial acquisition to the Order. In the Golden Bull of Rimini, the emperor 'confirmed' Konrad's donations and transferred Prussia into the direct sovereign possession of the Order. The document was backdated to 1226. The Teutonic Knights were no longer vassals of duke Konrad, but the sovereign owners of the lands of Chełmno and Michałow and whole Prussia.

1237 The Livonian Order united in a political-military alliance with the more powerful and privileged Teutonic Order. The idea was approved by both Pope Gregory IX and Emperor Frederick II.

On March 20, 1239, Herman von Salza dies. Although he never visited Prussia, during the 10 years of his reign, the Teutonic Knights conquered most of the Prussian tribes.

Summer 1239. The Teutonic Knights conquer Warmia aka Warmland.

1239. A Christian army composed of crusader knights from Masovia, Germany and all of Western Europe broke the resistance of the Natangians. The Crusaders signed a peace treaty that obliged the defeated and subjugated Prussians to fight the pagans on the side of the Teutonic Knights. Refusal was to be punishable by death. Out of the subdued Natangians, the Order formed faithful units of first local knights and retainers. As a guarantee of keeping the treaty, the Teutonic Knights demanded the sons of the Prussian nobles as hostages.

1239. Duke of Gdansk Pomerania Świętopełk started a war for control over the lower Vistula River. First, he built the stronghold of Sartowice and began to collect duty from the Teutonic ships and their subjects, then he started seizing German shipping on the Vistula. Finally, he stopped all shipping and cut off the Teutonic strongholds of the interior from their supplies. At that time, the Vistula River together with the Nogat was an important communication route of military, strategic and commercial importance, as it connected Toruń and Chełmno Land with the Teutonic castles in Prussia and provided the Order with access to the sea and seaborne assistance.

1242 At the instigation of the papal legate, William of Modena, the Teutonic Knights invaded northern Ruthenia, bloodied by wars with the Swedes and Genghis Khan's Mongols Golden Horde!

On April 5, 1242, a battle was fought on the frozen Lake Peipus. The Ruthenian forces under the command of the Novgorod prince Alexander numbered about 15,000 knights and retainers, and the Order's army was 10,000 strong. The battle ended in the complete defeat of the Order's forces. Many Teutonic knights died in the Peipus' icy waters, while 50 brother-knights were taken prisoner. Duke Alexander Nevsky stopped for good any notions of the Teutonic expansion to the east into the northern Ruthenia.

In the winter of 1243, a unit of the Teutonic Knights under the command of Dytrich von Bernheim, the Marshal of the Prussian province, captured the Pomeranian Sartowice castle by deceit, murdering and slaughtering the old men, women and children staying there.

On February 7, 1249, a treaty was concluded in Dzierzgoń between the Prussian tribes and the Teutonic Order through the papal legate Jacob of Leodium that obliged the Prussians to observe the Christian religion and renounce pagan beliefs and rites. The Pope took the Prussians and their land under his special protection. The Prussians had to give up polygamy, were to keep Sundays holy and to rebuild all the churches destroyed during the uprising. The treaty imposed the obligation on the Prussians to pay tithes and forced military service for the Teutonic Knights. In return, the Prussians received personal freedom, the right to inherit property and equal rights with the German settler population. If they renounced Christianity, however, they were to lose all privileges and freedom. Duke Świętopełk of Gdansk Pomerania retained his duchy, but had to give the Teutonic Knights his possessions east of the Vistula River and provide them with duty-free shipping at his port of Danzig, all without tariffs. The conquered territories were to be colonized by the Teutonic Knights by settlers brought from Mazovia, Bohemia and Germany.

1250 In the first half of the 13th century, the Lithuanian Prince Mindowe united the tribes of upper Lithuania and began expansion into the lands of Samogitia and Ruthenia. To prevent him from doing so, the Teutonic Knights formed a coalition against him. Acting on the threat Mindowe turned the tables and concluded an alliance with the Order and was even baptized in 1250. By 1253 he was crowned King of Lithuania by the new Lithuanian Bishop, who was a Teutonic priest, named Christian.

1255 the Teutonic Knights attacked Sambia and Samogitia, which lay between the Order's lands in Prussia and Livonia. The forces of the Order led by the Grand Master Poppon von Ostern, the Prussian Bishops of Warmia and Chełmno, and the crusaders: Czechs and Germans, led by the Czech king Ottokar II and Otto, the margrave of Brandenburg, defeated the Sambians. The crusaders slaughtered the Sambian people so much that the elders voluntarily handed over hostages to Ottokar II so that the Christians would not exterminate the whole tribe. Sambia was ravaged, and what could not be taken was destroyed and burned.

In 1256, an anti-Teutonic uprising broke out in Sambia, but was quickly and bloodily suppressed. The Sambians promised to be baptized and submit to the rule of the Order. In honor of the Czech king, on the right bank of the Pregoła river, a mile from its mouth to the sea, a castle was built called Königsberg. An urban settlement was soon built nearby. The Teutonic knights secured the loyalty of the Sambian nobles by granting them considerable fiefs with peasants, who from then on became subjects of their tribes.

1258 The conquest of Sambia was finally completed. The land of formerly free people was divided between the Teutonic Order and the bishop residing in Königsberg. The Sambia bishop received a third of the land.

Summer 1260. The Teutonic Knights organize a great raid on Samogitia. Among the crusaders is the Mazovian prince, Siemowit I.

1260 Mindowe broke the alliance with the Teutonic Knights and abandoned Christianity. The Teutonic bishopric of Lithuania ceased to exist.

1260 Lithuanians took revenge on the Masovian Poles for their participation in the expedition to Samogitia. Mendowe forces ravaged Mazovia, killed Prince Siemowit I and took his son, future Konrad II, prisoner.

January 1260. Pope Alexander IV allowed the Teutonic Knights to take hostages from among the Prussians who did not want to build strongholds or did not support the Order with arms and military service. This was a clear violation of the Dzierzgon agreement! The Teutonic Knights also received permission to accept into their ranks anyone who applied for it and began a large-scale recruitment campaign throughout Christian Europe

July 1260. The defeat of the Teutonic Knights in the Battle of Lake Durbe signaled the outbreak of the Second Prussian Uprising. The Prussians began to abandon the Christian religion en masse. The bishops of Sambia and Warmia left their dioceses, and the entire clergy fled with them. Almost all the Prussian tribes between the Niemen and the Vistula Rivers embraced the fight and joined the uprising. The uprising high commanders had been trained in the army of the Order. The Sambians were commanded by Glende, the Natangs by Herkus Monte, the Warmians by Glappo, the Pogezans by Autume, and the Bartoms by Dziwan. Both sides knew their enemies very well, their ways of fighting and weapons. The insurgents quickly took over the countryside and began to besiege the isolated strongholds.

On January 22, 1261, the battle of Pokarvis took place. In several clashes, the Prussians led by Herkus Monte destroyed two large but separate crusaders divisions: the first under the command of Count Barba that had been directed to fight in Sambia, the second under the command of Count Reyden was to conquer Natanga.

Beginning of 1263, the Natangs commanded by Monte invaded the Chełmno Land. According to the Teutonic chronicler Peter of Dusburg, Monte made it red with the blood of Christians.

At the same time, a unit of Yotvingians led by Skumand reached Toruń, while another entered Pomezania and destroyed Kwidzyn. On the way back, the battle of Lubawa took place, in which Monte's army defeated the Teutonic troops, led by the national champion Helmeric von Wurzburg. Forty battle-hardened brothers died, and with them almost the entire Christian army. It was the greatest defeat of the Teutonic Order during the Prussian crusades.

1265 - Pope Clement IV announced a crusading expedition to Prussia. It was attended by Albrecht, Duke of Brunswick, and Albrecht, Duke of Thuringia. Their armies attacked Sambia.

1267/68 - At the turn of 1267 and 1268, the king Premysl II Ottokar of Bohemia, came to the Baltic Sea. His army was sent to Natangia. Another crusader, Otto III of Brandenburg, operated on the Warmia-Natang coast.

Autumn of 1273. In the Stabława Forest, the Teutonic Knights captured and hanged Herkus Monte, who led the Prussians to fight the Order for the freedom of his people.

1274. The Second Prussian Uprising finally collapsed. The Prussians who were taken prisoner lost everything and became slaves. Many of them were employed to rebuild old castles and build new, now of stone, Teutonic fortresses. Prussian nobles who did not take part in the uprising or surrendered voluntarily kept their estates and even received lands from the Teutonic Knights along with the peasant population living there. From these nobles the Prussian nobility would later emerge.

1274-1278 - the Teutonic Knights conquered two Prussian tribes: the Nadra and the Skala, and in 1278 they began to deal with the Yotvingians. After five years of constant raids, campaigns and invasions, one of the tribes, numbering about 1,500 warriors, accepted the Order's rule, agreeing to the Teutonic garrisons and degrading themselves to the role of the Order's vassals. However, most of the Yotvingians were resettled to Pomerania, Pogezania and Sambia. The rest fled to Samogitia and Lithuania, where they joined numerous Prussian refugees already there: Barts, Skalans, Nadrans and Pogezans. On the devastated no man's land, which separated the Teutonic possessions from Lithuania, the Teutonic Knights built defensive strongholds. From there, using the services of the Christianized Prussians, they conducted a raiding war against Lithuania, penetrating deeply into its territory.

August 1308. Brandenburg margraves: Otto IV and Valdemar, entered the area of Gdańsk Pomerania and began the siege of the city of Gdańsk. Duke Wladyslaw I Łokietek, ruler of Gdansk Pomerania had been busy in the south of his Polish realm and by the Brandenburgian invasion lost access to the Baltic Sea, in turn ordered Judge Bogusza to ask the Teutonic Order, his ally, for help. The Teutonic army, under the command of Günter von Schwarzeburg, together with the Poles drove the Brandenburgers out of Gdańsk. As a guarantee that duke Wladyslaw I would settle his financial obligations towards the Order, the Teutonic Knights took a group of Polish magnates' hostage, including Judge Bogusz and Castellan Wojciech.

On November 13, 1308, the Teutonic Knights massacred Polish townspeople and knights in Gdańsk. According to various sources, from several dozen to several hundred people were killed.

The Order commenced to take over the Gdansk Pomerania lands. Władysław Łokietek did not have enough strength to immediately take up arms against the Order.

In the same year 1308, the Bishop of Riga, deprived of power by the Teutonic Knights, in the hope of regaining it, turned to Clement V with a request to dissolve the Teutonic Order, accusing the brothers of living in luxury, promiscuity and cruelty. Soon after, accusations of sodomy and witchcraft appeared against them.

1309 - wanting to avoid the fate of the Templars, the Grand Master of the Teutonic Order moved the main seat of the Teutonic Order from Venice to Malbork, making it the capital of the Teutonic state.

In January 1309, duke Władysław II demanded the return of Gdańsk Pomerania from the Teutonic master in exchange for financial compensation, but the amount of one hundred thousand grzywna demanded by the Teutonic Knights was far beyond Wladyslaw II's capabilities.

On September 3, 1309, Waldemar, Margrave of Brandenburg, sold his 'imaginary' rights to Gdańsk Pomerania to the Teutonic Knights, and soon after, the besieged stronghold of Świecie surrendered to the Order, finalizing the Teutonic conquest of Gdansk Pomerania. As a result, Poland lost direct access to the sea for over 150 years.

Autumn 1324, in Brześć Kujawski, at the Polish-Teutonic congress, king of Poland Władysław II Łokietek demanded the return of the areas of Gdańsk Pomerania and Chełmno Land from the Teutonic Knights. The deputies of the newly elected commander Werner von Orseln rejected these demands. For their part, they offered Łokietek 10,000 Grzywna and some of their possessions in Kyjawy/Kuyavia for renouncing his rights to

Gdansk Pomerania. The Polish monarch rejected these proposals.

1327-28– king Władysław I Łokietek made an unsuccessful attempt to obtain homage from the Mazovian dukes who supported the Order. When Siemowit II, Trojden I and Wacław of Płock refused, Łokietek decided to undertake military action. In this way, he started another Polish-Teutonic war. Polish crown army was battling Masovian armies, Teutonic divisions and king of Bohemia John of Luxembourg's army.

December 1328. The troops led by John of Luxembourg marched through Polish territory, heading for Königsberg, where troops were concentrated before the expedition against Lithuania.

1329-1332 Polish-Order war - The Teutonic Knights aided by John of Luxemburg ravaged Wielkopolska, captured Dobrzyn Land and Kujawy.

On February 1, 1329, John of Luxembourg and the Teutonic Knights ravaged Samogitia. At that time, Władysław II Łokietek entered the area of Chełmno.

On September 27, 1331, the Polish Crown army won their first field victory against the army of the Teutonic Order in the great battle of Płowce. The battle went back and forth and Władysław II Łokietek, fearing for the life of the heir to the throne, ordered Prince Casimir to leave the battlefield, which was used by the Teutonic propaganda, spreading to all and sundry that the prince did it out of cowardice.

On April 21, 1332, the Teutonic Knights captured Brześć Kujawski, and on April 26 Inowrocław. Soon after, the Teutonic Order occupied all of Kujawy.

On August 26, 1332, John of Luxembourg, who styled himself the King of Bohemia and Poland, granted the right to Kujawy to the Order, which they had already conquered.

On November 26, 1335, a trial was held and verdict was announced in the Polish-Teutonic territorial dispute. King Casimir III the Great was to regain Kujawy and the Dobrzyń Land, and the Order was to keep all earlier grants in this area. Gdansk Pomerania was to remain in the hands of the Order.

In the summer of 1336, Casimir the Great sent a complaint to Pope Benedict XII against the Teutonic Order, for non-payment of the compensation awarded to Polish Crown in 1321 for Gdańsk Pomerania. The King of Poland promised the Holy See half of the recovered amount.

On July 22, 1338, Louis IV of Wittelsbach forbade the Teutonic Knights to cede any territories to Poland and Lithuania, and also forbade the Order to appear before the papal court without his consent.

On September 8, 1338, the Papal Judge Galhard de Carceribus was authorized to collect the compensation awarded on February 10, 1321 to king Władysław II Łokietek from the Teutonic Order. Of the awarded amount of 30,000 Grzywna, half was to become a donation to the Holy See.

September 15, 1339 in the Church of St. John in Warsaw, the verdict of the papal court was announced, according to which the Order was to give back all unjustly seized lands, including Gdańsk Pomerania, and pay compensation. The verdict remained on paper and acquired only propaganda significance.

On July 8, 1343, in Kalisz, king Casimir III the Great concluded an agreement with the Teutonic Order. The king was to receive compensation in the amount of 10,000 florins in gold and regain Kujawy and the Dobrzyń lands. In return, he renounced Pomerania and the Chełmno and Michałow lands with the towns of Orłowo, Nieszawa and Murzyn.

In the summer of 1349, Casimir III the Great concluded a border treaty with the Teutonic Order.

On September 16, 1349, Clement VI commissioned King Casimir to complete the process of Christianization of Lithuania.

1351 - 1355 future King Władysław II Jagiellon (Jogaila) was born to Duke Olgerdus, grandson of duke Gedeminnus. The boy grew up in Vilnius at his father's court, where he spent a lot of time with his cousin, Vitoldus.

1356 - In the second half of 1356, Casimir III the Great concluded a peace treaty with the Lithuanians.

1357 - Casimir III the Great strove for the Christianization of Lithuania by Poland and for its incorporation into the Polish ecclesiastical province.

May 1377. After the death of his father, Duke Jogaila took power in the Grand Duchy of Lithuania. Duke Jogaila then received a seal depicting the prince in armor, with a sword in his hand, sitting on a horse and rushing to the right. This image later became the ancestral coat of arms of the Jagiellonian dynasty. Jogaila maintained his power in Lithuania mainly thanks to the considerable help of his uncle Kinstut.

August - September 1377. The Teutonic Grand Master Winrich von Kniprode, accompanied by duke Albrecht III Habsburg, invaded and mercilessly ravaged Samogitia with two thousand cavalry, and the Livonian Master with yet another large forces besieged Novum Castrum Rutenorum located near Daugavpils.

1379 - On September 29, 1379, Dukes Jogaila and Kinstut Gedeminnovich concluded a ten-year truce with the Teutonic Order, however, the treaty did not cover the territory of Samogitia.

1380 - On May 31, 1380, Duke Jogaila concluded a treaty with Grand Master Winrich von Kniprode, in which he undertook not to support Duke Kinstut during the Teutonic expeditions to his district of Lithuanian lands.

1382 - May 1382, Jogaila's brother, Dmitry Koribut, the duke of Seversk, raised a rebellion. Duke Kinstut ended the fight with the Teutonic Knights and summoned duke Jogiala to participate in the punitive expedition. However, instead of waiting for his nephew, he himself set out to extinguish the rebellion in the Seversk Land. Jogaila took advantage of this unexpected smile of fate, communicated with the Vilnius townspeople and concluded a settlement with them, promising to conclude peace with the Teutonic Knights, which they wanted very much, as they drew huge profits from trade with Riga. On June 12, Jogaila returned to the throne in Vilnius and regained control of Lithuania.

July 6, 1382. Kinstut went to Samogitia for armed support. Meanwhile, the Teutonic army reached Trakai and negotiations began, in which the Lithuanians were represented by prince Schirgalo. As a result, at Brazoła, Jogaila concluded a truce with the Teutonic Order, under which he promised not to support Kinstut with arms.

On November 1, 1382, on the Dubissa River, Jogaila concluded a four-year truce with the Order. He gave them Samogitia as far as Dubissa, promised to support the Order militarily and to be baptized.

1383 - On July 30, 1383, Grand Master Konrad Zöllner von Rotenstein declared war on Jogaila.

August 1383. Grand Master Konrad Zöllner von Rotenstein entered Lithuania accompanied by Vitoldus Kinstutovich, joined by faithful Samogitians. On September 12, 1383, he captured Trakai and then laid siege to Vilnius.

1384 - July 1384 Duke Jogiala concluded a pact with his cousin Vitoldus. Vitoldus betrayed the

Teutonic Knights, burned Marienborg castle, and then returned to Vilnius. As a reward, Duke Jogaila gave him Podlasie, Grodno, Wołkowysk, Kamieniec and Brest.

In September 1384, the Lithuanians marched on Neu-Marienwerder and on November 6, 1384, the Teutonic fortress surrendered.

On October 16, 1384, Princess Jadwiga of Anjou, granddaughter of Casimir III the Great, was crowned Queen of Poland by Archbishop Boędza.

1385 - On January 18, 1385, Jadwiga of Anjou received Jogaila's embassy, who made her a marriage proposal. One of the Lithuanian newcomers was prince Schirgalo.

January - February 1385. After accepting the marriage of Jadwiga of Anjou with Jogaila, the Polish magnates sent delegates to her mother Queen Elizabeth of Bosnia asking for the marriage's blessing.

August 1385. Teutonic troops entered the Lithuanian lands again. Prince Vitoldus and Schirgalo repulsed Teutonic attacks on the Niemen River.

On August 14, 1385, in Krewo, the Grand Duke of Lithuania Jogaila issued a document known as the Union of Krewo. The act was a promise and took the form of a prenuptial agreement. It was the result of long-term negotiations between the Lithuanian and Polish sides, as well as Queen Elizabeth of Bosnia, the mother of queen Jadwiga. Duke Jogaila undertook to accept Christianity in the Catholic rite together with his family, court and nobles, and to free Poles taken captive by his armies and residing in Lithuanian realms. He also undertook to pay prince Wilhelm Habsburg 200,000 florins as compensation for the broken engagement with Queen Jadwiga. In addition, Jogaila promised to join his Lithuanian and Ruthenian lands to the Kingdom of Poland.

1385-6 The union of Lithuania and Poland was concluded. Lithuania was baptized in the Latin rite.

February 1386 On his way to Kraków, Grand Duke Jogaila stopped in Sandomierz, from where he sent a request to Konrad Zöllner von Rotenstein that the Grand Master be his godfather.

On February 12, 1386, twelve-year-old Jadwiga of Anjou welcomed thirty-five-year-old Jogaila who had arrived in Kraków from Lithuania.

February 15, 1386 Jadwiga participated in the solemn baptism of Jogaila, who took the name Władysław, and since then would be known as Wladyslaw II Jagiellon.

February 18, 1386 Queen Jadwiga of Anjou marries Władysław The wedding was officiated by Archbishop Boędza.

On March 4, 1386, Władysław Jagiellon was crowned King-consort of Poland and who became Wladyslaw II.

March 1386. the royal couple Jadwiga of Anjou and Władysław II Jagiellon accepted the homage of the Lithuanian princes and prince Siemowit I, Piast ruler of Duchy of Masovia.

On May 22, 1386, Władysław II Jagiellon approved the agreement concluded by prince Schirgalo with the widow of Sviatoslav of Smolensk, under which her son George Sviatoslvovitz sat on the Smolensk throne.

At the end of May 1386, Jadwiga of Anjou and Władysław II Jagiellon received the Pope's envoy, Archbishop Maffiolus, in Kraków, who took their oath of allegiance to the Holy See.

On July 10, 1386, in Lębork, Grand Master Konrad Zöllner von Rotenstein built a coalition against Poland and Lithuania, which included the Western Pomeranian princes Vartislav VII and Bogislav VIII.

February 1387 In order to return the lands of Galician or Red Ruthenia to Poland, queen Jadwiga of Anjou marched her Crown army on an expedition accompanied by many magnates and lords of her kingdom, among others: Dobiesław of Kurozwęki, Spytko II of Melsztyn, Sędziwój of Szubin and Jan of Tarnów.

On February 20, 1387, a general congress of the Lithuanian nobles aka boyars began in Vilnius. King Władysław II Jagiellon undertook to bring all Lithuanians to the Catholic faith. In addition, the king granted Lithuanian magnates and the Catholic Church a number of privileges, including the guarantee of ownership of their native lands and the right to freely marry off their daughters, while the Church in Lithuania was exempted from state taxes.

On March 6, 1387, queen Jadwiga of Anjou arrived in Lwow, where she confirmed the earlier rights (also of residents of different nationalities) and privileges of the townspeople, abolished customs duties and tributes, and granted the city the right of storage.

In the spring of 1387, King Władysław II Jagiellon began the general baptism of Lithuanians. During the tour of Lithuanian Duchy, the people gathered in the more important towns, where they were baptized en masse.

On April 17, 1387, in a bull, Pope Urban VI called Władysław II Jagiellon a treasure hidden and found.

On April 28, 1387, Jagiełło made Schirgalo his governor in Lithuania.

August 1387. Jadwiga of Anjou's expedition was a complete success, and Red Ruthenia was permanently annexed to Poland.

1387 In Volhynia, Prince Vitoldus met Prince Vasyl, the heir to the Moscow throne. Władysław II Jagiellon, learning about this and knowing the ease with which Vitoldus made and broke alliances, forbade him any contact with the rulers of the Grand Duchy of Muscovy.

1387. Under pressure from Polish magnates, Władysław II Jagiellon handed over part of Volhynia and the land of Łuck to the administration of the Crown Starosts. The Lithuanian magnates did not like it.

On December 3, 1387, Jadwiga of Anjou reminded the authorities of Kraków that the homage of loyalty paid to her in 1384 was also due to her consort, King Władysław II Jagiellon.

Summer of 1388. The canonical process against Jadwiga of Anjou and Władysław II Jagiełło came to an end. The verdict confirmed the legality of their marriage, but despite this, Jadwiga's former fiancé, Wilhelm Habsburg, still considered himself her legal spouse and remained unmarried until her death.

In August 1388, Władysław II Jagiellon concluded an agreement with Emperor Sigismund of Luxemburg, and the following month the knight Ekhard von dem Walde joined the anti-Teutonic alliance, endowed with two villages in the Poznań region.

In the spring of 1389, Władysław II Jagiellon placed his brother Simeon Lingwen on the throne of Novgorod.

1389 - On June 6, 1389, during the next round of negotiations between Polish envoys with the deputies of the Teutonic Order, negotiations broke off in Nidzica. It happened when the Teutonic deputies demanded permission to confirm the rights of the Teutonic Order to the Lithuanian lands, presenting the act of granting those rights by the emperor and the pope as evidence.

In October 1389, Grand Master Konrad Zöllner complained in a letter to Jadwiga of Anjou against her husband Władysław Jagiełło that he still supported Lithuanians and Ruthenians in the fight against the Order.

Autumn 1389 During Duke Schirgalo's absence, Prince Vitoldus tried to take Vilnius, and only thanks to Dimitry Koribut's vigilance this effort failed.

On December 10, 1389, an alliance between Władysław II Jagiełłon and the Wallachian Hospodar Mircza the Old was concluded in Radom.

At the end of 1389, Władysław Opolczyk guaranteed a loan to Władysław Jagiełło in the amount of 500 marks, taken from Lewek, a Jewish man from Kraków.

At the turn of January and February 1390, a powerful Teutonic army set out from Prussia and entered the territory of Lithuania. At Marshal Rabe's side stood Prince Vitoldus, thus starting the second war with now King Wladyslaw II Jagiellon.

1390 - February 1390. In retaliation for Vitoldus' actions, Władysław II Jagiellon invaded his strongholds: Brest and Kamieniec Litewski (where the ranks of king's army were joined by a group of 900 volunteers). Soon after, the city surrendered to the Polish king.

March-April 1390. Władysław II Jagiełłon with the Polish knights set off to Grodno to recapture the city recently seized by the Teutonic Knights.

Spring 1390 After the start of the war with the Teutonic Order, Władysław II Jagiełłon asked Pope Boniface IX for help in concluding an agreement. The Pope sent his representative to Kraków and Malbork, accompanied by the Neapolitan knight Ludwik.

1390 Jadwiga of Anjou resumed the activities of the Jagiellonian University.

1391 - On March 12, 1391, Konrad Wallenrod was elected the new Grand Master of the Teutonic Order in Malbork.

On April 8, 1391, during the absence of Władysław Jagiełło, Jadwiga of Anjou took on the responsibilty of managing the kingdom and managed to bring about a meeting of the Polish legation headed by Sędziwoj from Szubin, with representatives of the Order.

On June 28, 1391, Duke Władysław of Opole pledged the town of Złotoria to the Teutonic Knights.

On July 13, 1391, Jadwiga of Anjou and the Starost of Kraków, Spytek of Melsztyn, asked Duke Władysław of Opole through deputies, about the reason why he pledged Złotoria to the Teutonic Knights.

On July 22, 1391, Władysław II Jagiełłon promised his brother Skirgielle that he would never give up Vilnius, Vitebsk, Grodno and Merecz without his knowledge.

On August 15, 1391, Władysław II Jagiełłon seized the castle in Raciążek, which at that time belonged to Duke Henry VIII of Legnica. The war began with Duke Władysław Opolczyk.

To help the Lithuanians in the fight against the Teutonic Knights and Vytautas, Władysław II Jagiełłon sent food and armaments from Poland to his homeland.

1392 - Władysław II Jagiello's brother Prince Simeon Lingwen resigned from the throne of Novgorod. The immediate cause of the abdication was pressure from Moscovy.

In the spring of 1392, Duke Henry of Mazovia went to Prussia on a secret mission. Under the guise of brokering peace talks between Poland and the Teutonic Order, he was to reconcile King Wladysaw II with Prince Vitoldus.

On June 28, 1392, after the death of Duke Władysław of Opole's son-in-law, Wigunt-Alexander, Inowroclaw Kuyavia should have been returned to the Opole's prince. This did not happen, because his daughter's dowry, the Inowroclaw Kuyavia, was taken by Władysław II Jagiełło.

On July 4, 1392, an agreement was concluded in Ostrów with Vitoldus ending the long-term conflict with his cousin, the king. He received his patrimony in Lithuania and pledged allegiance to the Queen and King of Poland.

On July 27, 1392, Duke Władysław of Opole pledged the lands of Dobrzyń Land to Grand Master Konrad von Wallenrode for the amount of 50,000 Hungarian florins. On August 10, in Bobrowniki, the Duke of Opole released his subjects from the oath of allegiance, and the Grand Master accepted such an oath. Only the inhabitants of Dobrzyń town and castle, who defended themselves until August 16, 1392, put up any resistance in the Dobrzyn Land.

In September 1392, Duke Władysław of Opole proposed to Konrad von Wallenrode that the Order joined the anti-Polish coalition, which would include: emperor Sigismund of Luxemburg, Margrave Jodok, duke Jan of Zgorzelec, Duke Albrecht III Habsburg and King Venceslaus IV of Bohemia. The coalition's task would be to overthrow Władysław II Jagiellon and divide the Kingdom of Poland.

1393 - Beginning of 1393, the youngest brother of Władysław II, Swidrigelo, ordered the murder of ducal governor Viesna and seized power in the Duchy of Vitebsk. The Polish King ordered Schirgelo and Vitoldus to undertake an expedition to suppress the rebellion.

In 1393, Władysław II Jagiellon entered into an alliance with the Tatar Khan Tokhtamysh.

1396 - On May 28, 1396, the ruler of Wallachia, Vlad, declared himself a vassal of Polish rulers Władysław II Jagiellon and Jadwiga of Anjou.

On July 14, 1396, the army of King Władysław II Jagiellon entered the territory of the Duchy of Opole, starting the third war with Duke Władysław of Opole. Thanks to the mediation of Polish magnates, it ended on August 6.

1397 - June 10-19, 1397 Queen Jadwiga of Anjou met in Włocławek with the Master of the Teutonic Order, Konrad von Jungingen, and started negotiations on the recovery of Dobrzyń Land by Polish Crown.

1398 - May 1398. In Toruń, negotiations took place between queen Jadwiga of Anjou and Count Jan von Seyn regarding the recovery of Dobrzyń Land by the Crown but they ended in failure.

On October 12, 1398, on the island of Salin on the Neman River, Prince Vitoldus concluded an agreement with the Teutonic Order, which disturbed both King Władysław II and Polish magnates. Vitoldus, in exchange for help in conquering Novgorod the Great, renounced Samogitia (and even offered the Teutonic Knights support in its conquest) and resigned from his claims to Pskov. He allowed not only the expansion of the Order's state, but also the outflanking of Duchy of Lithuania from the west and north.

1399 - July 1399 Queen Of Poland Jadwiga of Anjou dictated her last will, in which she allocated most of her private funds to the University of Kraków. For this, among others, a house was purchased, which became the nucleus of Collegium Maius, and a building for the College of Law and Medicine at the Grodzka Street.

On July 17, 1399, the Polish Queen and ruler Jadwiga died upon giving birth to a daughter who also died.

On August 12, 1399, in the Battle of the Vorskla River, the combined Lithuanian-Ruthenian-Polish-Teutonic army, supported by Khan Tokhtamysh' Tatars, was routed by the Golden Horde Tatar army of Edigu and Temur Qutlug. Many knights fell in the battle, including lord Spytko of Melsztyn, master of Podolia. Upon hearing of the defeat, King Wladyslaw II Jagiellon ordered the fords and crossings on the Dnieper River manned with an army.

1400 - December 1400 King Władysław II Jagiellon gave Vitoldus lifelong powers in Duchy of Lithuania, on the condition that after his death without issue they would revert to the Crown of the Kingdom of Poland.

1401 - On January 18, 1401, Prince Vitoldus Kinstutovich, who called himself the Prince of Lithuania, issued a document in Vilnius confirming his loyalty to the Polish Crown and the king.

On March 11, 1401, the Polish royal council gathered in Radom agreed to Vitoldus' assuming the grand duke's powers in Lithuanian duchy, as well as to the additional condition of the boyars that in the event of Wladyslaw II's childless death, the Poles would not elect a king without their consent. This arrangement was called the Union of Vilnius and Radom.

1402- On May 24, 1402, King Władysław II Jagellon and prince Swidrigelo together with the royal retinue went to Toruń for a convention concerning the return of Dobrzyń Land to the Polish kingdom and the retaining of Samogitia by the Order.

1404 - In Raciążek, King Władysław II Jagiellon negotiated with the Teutonic Order the possibility of regaining Dobrzyń Land, pledged to the Order by Duke Władysław of Opole in 1392.

1409-1410 - On August 16, 1409, the Polish-Teutonic war broke out, interrupted on October 8 with the signing of a truce until June 24, 1410. The Teutonic army occupied the Dobrzyń Land, captured towns and strongholds of Dobrzyń, Rypin, Lipno, Bobrowniki, Złotorja and Bydgoszcz. Also, the borderland of the Duke of Masovia were on fire.

24-30th of June 1410 – king's armies crossed the Vistula River over the pontoon bridge at Czewinsk, joined by the Lithuanian-Ruthenian army and Masovian dukes' army.

On July 3, 1410 the king's armies started marching towards the Teutonic State borders, and on July 9 they crossed into Prussia. On July 11 King Wladyslaw II Jagiellon decided against crossing deeper into the Order realm near Kurzednik on Drweca River, and instead armies marched further east taking Dabrowno and then due north-east arriving near Grunwald on the evening of July 14.

On July 15, 1410, the army led by Władysław II Jagiełło and Prince Vytautas defeated the Teutonic Order in the Battle of Grunwald.

Robert Krzysztof Zareba

July 15, AD 2020

Short Biographies of the Principal Combatants

Wladislaus rex Polonie

Born in 1352 or 1363 into the Gediminid dynasty. He was originally named Jogaila and after his baptism took the name Władysław II Jagiełło. He was Grand Duke of Lithuania (1377–1434) and then King-consort of Poland (1386–1399) alongside his wife Queen Jadwiga until 1399 and then as King of Poland on his own (1399-1434). In 1387, he converted his Lithuanian state to Catholicism as part of the deal brokered by the ruling clans and leading aristocracy of both states at the Union of Krewo which once signed created a Polish-Lithuanian state, largest political entity in late 14th century Europe.

The Union accelerated the growing tensions between the Teutonic knights monastic state and Poland-Lithuania. As part of the terms Wladyslaw II Jagiełło promised to adopt Christianity with his subjects, but also the repatriation of lands "stolen" from Poland by its neighbors, and terras suas Lithuaniae et Russiae Coronae Regni Poloniae perpetuo applicare, which has been interpreted by some historians to mean anything from a personal union between Lithuania and Poland to a complete incorporation of Lithuania into Poland. Although the Polish-Lithuanian Kingdom tried to work with the Teutonic Knights on several occasions, once the Lithuanians converted to Christianity, the Order's war raids was not supposed to enter those territories.

Even though he was King or Poland and Grand Duke of Lithuania he had to maneuver between rebellious lords and hostile neighbors. At times he feuded with his cousin Vitoldus, but also relied on him over time. Ongoing battles between the Order and Lithuanian nobles and erroneous policies by duke Vitoldus resulted in loss of Samogitia in 1404. This in turn triggered attempts, clandestine and fueling rebellion, to regain the province in 1409. When the Order said they would act against the Samogitian rebels Poland's response was that they would intervene on behalf of the rebels. As a result, the Order issued a preemptive declaration of war against Poland which led to the great war and battle at Grunwald.

The allied victory at the Battle of Grunwald in 1410, followed by the Peace of Thorn, secured the Polish and Lithuanian borders and marked the emergence of the Polish–Lithuanian alliance as a significant force in central, eastern and south-eastern Europe.

In the Union of Horodło, signed on 2 October 1413, king decreed that the status of the Grand Duchy of Lithuania was "tied to our Kingdom of Poland permanently and irreversibly" and granted the Catholic nobles of Lithuania privileges equal to those of the Polish then solidifying noble class. The act included a clause prohibiting the Polish nobles from electing a monarch without the consent of the Lithuanian nobles, and the Lithuanian nobles from electing a grand duke without the consent of the Polish monarch and his nobles.

King Wladyslaw II Jagiełło fought or cause to be fought several subsequent wars against the Teutonic Order after 1411 through 1435 but he did not make the Prussian monistic state subservient to Polish realm until it was secularized in the 16th century when Albert of Prussia, kinsman of the Jagiellon dynasty, swore homage to Wladyslaw II Jagiełło's grandson Sigusmund I in 1525. When he died in 1434, he set the stage for the expansion of the Jagiellonian dynasty to play a major part on the thrones of Europe and ushered a "golden age of prosperity" for Poland and Lithuania.

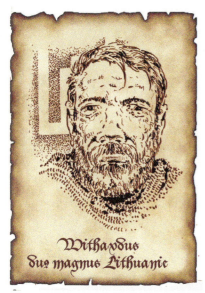

Alexander Vitoldus was also known as Vitoldus the Great was born in 1350 to the leading highest nobility of Duchy of Lithuania and was a cousin to king Wladyslaw II Jagiellon. From the late 14th century onwards, Vitoldus was a ruler of the Grand Duchy of Lithuania instead of the king. He was also the Prince of Grodno (1370–1382), Prince of Lutsk (1387–1389), and the proposed king of the Hussites.

Vitoldus' father Kinstut had jointly ruled the Grand Duke of Lithuania with his brother Olgerdus until his death in 1377. Olgerdus was succeeded by his son Jogaila, after which a power struggle for the throne ensued. Vitoldus and Kinstut were imprisoned, and Kinstut eventually was either killed or died. Vitoldus eventually escaped and he sought help from the Teutonic Order who were at war with Lithuania. Vitoldus was baptized as a Catholic for the first time, receiving the name of Wigand. Vitoldus participated in several raids against Jogaila. In January 1384, Vitoldus promised to cede part of Samogitia to the Teutonic Order, up to the Nevėžis River in return for recognition as Grand Duke of Lithuania. However, in July of the same year, Vitoldus broke with the Order and reconciled with Jogaila. He then burned three important Teutonic castles, and regained all Kinstut's lands, except for Trakai.

Vitoldus participated in the Union of Kewno agreements and in 1386 was re-baptized as a Catholic, receiving the name Alexander. Wladyslaw II Jagiello left his brother Schirgalo as his regent in Lithuania. However, Schirgalo was unpopular with the people and Vitoldus saw an opportunity to become the Grand Duke. In 1389, he attacked Vilnius but failed. In early 1390, Vitoldus again allied with the Teutonic Order through the Treaty of Königsberg (1390). He had to confirm his agreement of 1384 and cede Samogitia to the Order. In 1392, now Polish king Wladyslaw II offered to make Vitoldus regent instead of Schirgalo. Vitoldus accepted and again broke with the Order. He burned three Teutonic castles and returned to Vilnius. The king and duke signed the Astrava Treaty in which Vitoldus recovered all Kinstut's lands, including Trakai, and was given even more. He would rule Lithuania in the name of Wladyslaw II. After Vitoldus' death, all his lands and powers would revert to Wladyslaw II and his heirs.

Vitoldus continued Olgerdus' vision to expand to the east in the quest to regain as many Ruthenian lands as possible. Much of the territory was already under the Grand Duke's rule, but the rest was controlled by the Golden Horde Mongols. Tokhtamysh, Khan of the Golden Hord, sought help from Vitoldus when he had been removed from the throne in 1395 after his defeat by Timur. An agreement was reached that Vitoldus would help Tokhtamysh to regain power, and the Horde would cede more lands to the Grand Duchy of Lithuania in return. In 1398, Vitoldus' army attacked a part of the Crimea and built a castle there.

Vitoldus once again allied with the Order by the Treaty of Salynas in October 1398, Vitoldus, who now styled himself Supremus Dux Lithuaniae, ceded his ancestral province of Samogitia to the knights, formed an alliance with them for the conquest and partition of Pskov land and Novgorod the Great province.

Inspired by his successful campaign against Timur, Vitoldus and Wladyslaw II won support from Pope Boniface IX to organize a crusade against the Mongols. This political move also demonstrated that Lithuania had fully accepted Christianity and was defending the Christian faith on its own, and that the Teutonic Knights had no further basis for attacks against Lithuania. The campaign resulted in a crushing defeat of the crusaders at the Battle of the Vorskla River in 1399. Over twenty noble princes, including two brothers of king Wladyslaw II, were killed, and Vitoldus himself barely escaped alive. This came as a shock to the Grand Duchy of Lithuania and Poland. A number of territories revolted against Vitoldus, and Smolensk was retaken by its hereditary ruler, George of Smolensk, and not re-conquered by Lithuanians until 1404.

When the rebels in Samogitia rose in uprising and war against the Order broke out Vitoldus gathered a large host of his vassals, allies and subjects and joined Polish forces in the advance on Prussia. In 1410, Vitoldus himself commanded the forces of the Grand Duchy in the Battle of Grunwald. The battle ended in a decisive Polish-Lithuanian victory. Even though the subsequent siege of Marienburg, capital of the Order, was unsuccessful, the Teutonic Knights never regained their strength and from then on posed a much-reduced military threat to Poland-Lithuania.

As a result of the Peace of Thorn of 1411, Vitoldus received Samogitia for his lifetime. Vitoldus was one of the creators of the Union of Horodło with Poland in 1413. According to the acts of the union, the Grand Duchy of Lithuania was to retain a separate Grand Duke and its own council. At the same time both the Polish and Lithuanian Sejms were to discuss all the important matters jointly. This union was important culturally as well as politically because it granted Lithuanian Christian nobles the same rights as the Polish nobility already had. This act did not include the Orthodox nobles of the duchy. This paved the way for more contacts and cooperation between the nobles of Poland and Lithuania. Vitolduss died in the Trakai Island Castle, in 1430.

Zbigniew of Brzezie (or Zbigniew Lanckoroński) (ca. 1360 – ca. 1425) was a Polish lord, notable knight and nobleman of Zadora clan. Zbigniew served as Marshal of the Crown of Poland from 1399 to 1425 and starost of Kraków from 1409 to 1410. He was a diplomat and a close advisor to King Władysław II Jagiełło. He was an envoy making several legacies to the court of King of Hungary and Germany Sigismund of Luxembourg. During the Battle of Grunwald in 1410 he carried the Royal Pennon, and commanded the group a banners of the Marshal of the Crown group.

Ulrich von Jungingen was born in 1360 into the Swabian noble family and eventually he was elected the 26th Grand Master of the Teutonic Knights, serving from 1407 to 1410. His policy of confrontation with the Grand Duchy of Lithuania and the Kingdom of Poland would spark the Polish–Lithuanian–Teutonic Great War and lead to disaster for his Order, and his own death, at the Battle of Grunwald.

Ulrich and his elder brother Konrad von Jungingen, as younger sons excluded from succession in their family estates, took the monastic vows of the Teutonic Order and moved to the Teutonic State in Prussia. His career profited from the patronage of his elder brother Konrad, who was elected the Grand Master in 1393. Ulrich distinguished himself on several occasions in diplomatic negotiations.

In 1404 Ulrich was appointed the Order's Marshal (i.e. military leader) and Komtur – commander - of Königsberg. He had to deal with several Samogitian uprisings, which he fought both with strict violence and suppression and the bribery of the local nobles. Upon the sudden death of Grand Master Konrad von Jungingen in 1407, Ulrich was chosen as his successor on 26th of June 1407.

The new Grand Master had also inherited the growing conflict with King Wladyslaw II Jagiełło of Poland over the Dobrzyń Land and the pawned Neumark region. The Polish ambassador Archbishop Mikołaj Kurowski declared, that any attack on Lithuania aiding the rebels in Samogitia would inevitably entail an armed conflict with Poland. Despite the threat of a two-front war, Ulrich prepared for a preemptive strike. He forged an alliance with King Sigismund of Hungary, levied mercenaries in the Holy Roman Empire and invited many prominent Western knights as Order's guests in a new 'crusade' against the pagans of Poland and Lithuanian, and on 6th of August 1409 declared war against Poland.

Ulrich received no substantial military help from his ally King Sigismund, but more from Sigismund's brother King Wenceslaus IV of Bohemia, who even arranged a temporary truce and mediated between the belligerents, though eventually without a tangible result. On 2nd of July 1410, the Grand Master at the head of his army left his capital Marienburg, the Malbork Castle fortress, for the final battle against the united Polish and Lithuanian forces. Both sides met on 15th of July between the villages of Grunwald (Grünfelde) and Stębark (Tannenberg). As noontime approached, none of the armies made a move, until Ulrich, according to the annals of Jan Długosz, had two naked swords delivered to King Wladyslaw II Jagiełło with the insulting remark that the king and his cousin Vitoldus might live or die by them.

This act, seen as a bold provocation, sparked the Polish-Lithuanian acceptance of battle, begun by the advance of the Lithuanian wing that at first was repulsed by the Knights but soon followed by a second strike etc by king's forces. Battle luck changed, after Ulrich, sure of victory, decided to personally lead his remaining 16 reserve banners against the Polish troops hotly engaged in the combat. He nearly might have gotten his hold of the king, but missed that opportunity, and at the same time getting involved into the very fighting lost oversight of the entirety of the Order's military operations during the battle. After the allied Prussian forces of the Lizard Union under Nicholas von Renys broke away from the Order's forces, the Grand Master had to face then much superior numbers of the Polish-Lithuanian chivalry. When the returning Lithuanian banners attacked him from the rear, Ulrich's troops were routed and he himself was killed in action by a Polish knight. According to Polish chronicler Jan Długosz he dueled with and was defeated by Mszczuj of Skrzynno, Łabędź coat of arms. King Wladyslaw II arranged the transportation of his remains to Malbork Castle before he began the siege of Malbork.

Kuno was born in Franconia probably in 1360. He was a Great Commander of Order holding his office in the years 1404–1410. Before he took the office of the Great Commander, he was the Sambia vBailiff, the commander of Ragnety, the commander of Anger, the commander of Pokarmin, and the Great Hospitaller.

He was a trusted advisor to Grand Master Ulrich von Jungingen . He took part in the Battle of Grunwald, where commanded the right wing and he fought under the banner of Sztum. He died during the Battle of Grunwald.

Vogt -Bailiff - of Tczew (January 5, 1392 - June 18, 1393)

Commander in Ryn (April 2, 1394 - April 1396)

Cammander in Brodnica (May 1, 1396 - September 29, 1404)

Commander in Gniew (September 8, 1404 - July 3, 1407)

Commander in Königsberg (July 21, 1407 - July 15, 1410)

Frederick von Wallenrode was the brother of the Grand Master Conrad von Wallenrode, his relative was also Johann von Wallenrode, during 1393-1416 the metropolitan archbishop of Riga. Before 1393, Frederick von Wallenrode was the Bailiff of Tczew. At that time, Frederick's brother, the Grand Master of the Teutonic Order, Conrad von Wallenrode, also conducted lively economic and colonization activities within their Prussian realm. On his initiative, in 1393, a new commandery was established with its seat in Ryn. Its first head was Friedrich von Wallenrode. Later (after 1396) he was also the commander of Gniew, Brodnica and finally Królewiec/Konigsberg. Being the commander of Königsberg, he thus served as the Grand Marshal of the Teutonic Order. In the Battle of Grunwald, Frederick Wallenrode commanded the left wing of the Order's army.

About the Author

Mariusz Moroz was born in 1968. He lives in Poland in a beautiful town among green woods and silver lakes. Mariusz is a great enthusiast of action films, comic books and horses. He has been interested in history, especially focusing on the medieval era and the Teutonic Knights. He has drawn comics since childhood.

His published works:

1. *Mrs Twardowska ... and other stories* (2016)
2. *Cursed Wilderness 1280* (2017)
3. *Endorf* (2018)
4. *On the Battlefields of Grunwald* (2020)
5. *The Banners in the battle of Grunwald* (2020)

There are more works in progress

Feel free to contact him at: m.moroz@poczta.fm

Look for more books from Winged Hussar Publishing, LLC – E-books, paperbacks and Limited-Edition hardcovers. The best in history, science fiction and fantasy at:

https://www. wingedhussarpublishing.com

https://www.whpsupplyroom.com

or follow us on Facebook at:

Winged Hussar Publishing LLC

Or on twitter at:

WingHusPubLLC

For information and upcoming publications

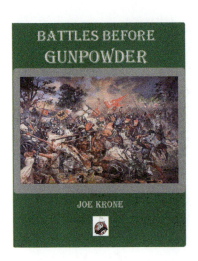

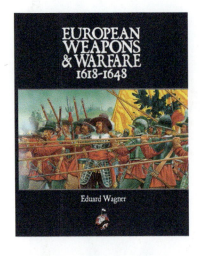
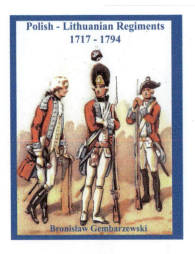